Smartphone Video Storytelling

Robb Montgomery

Routledge
Taylor & Francis Group

NEW YORK AND LONDON

First published 2018
by Routledge
711 Third Avenue, New York, NY 10017

and by Routledge
2 Park Square, Milton Park, Abingdon, Oxon, OX14 4RN

Routledge is an imprint of the Taylor & Francis Group, an informa business

Library of Congress Cataloging-in-Publication Data
Names: Montgomery, Robb, 1964- author.
Title: Smartphone video storytelling / Robb Montgomery.
Description: New York : Routledge, 2018.
Identifiers: LCCN 2017059607| ISBN 9781138635975 (hardback) |
    ISBN 9781138635999 (pbk.) | ISBN 9781315206288 (ebk.)
Classification: LCC PN19923926.A87 M66 2018 | DDC 791.4502/32—dc23
LC record available at https://lccn.loc.gov/2017059607

ISBN: 978-1-138-63597-5 (hbk)
ISBN: 978-1-138-63599-9 (pbk)
ISBN: 978-1-315-20628-8 (ebk)

Typeset in Bembo
by Apex CoVantage, LLC
Printed by CPI Group (UK) Ltd, Croydon CR0 4YY

Visit the website: www.SmartFilmSchool.com

For my daughters Kelli and Kayla … and the next generation of storytellers.

Contents

Online Examples

This book references 28 online examples that were filmed in 10 countries. These are viewable online at www.SmartFilmBook.com.

CHAPTER 1

- A big electronics show in Berlin

CHAPTER 2

- Video profile in Singapore
- Vertical video in Paris
- Olya in Lviv

CHAPTER 3

- Bild—No news photos in the newspaper?
- Unboxing a Beastgrip Pro and Moondog Labs lens

CHAPTER 4

- What is inside Egypt's pyramids?
- By the numbers
- BBC—An avalanche of ethics

CHAPTER 5

- Salad—shoot and edit a recipe
- Make a title card sequence
- Assemble a video postcard
- A studio approach to food shots

CHAPTER 6

- Newsmakers in Perugia
- The innovators

CHAPTER 7

- Breaking news—fire
- Live studio gear test

CHAPTER 8

- Am I awake?
- Making of "The ABC Song"

CHAPTER 9

- 360° surf school
- 5 tips for filming in 360°

CHAPTER 10

- Flamingo sunrise
- Across the Alps
- Ocean waves

CHAPTER 11

- Personal appeal—online instructor pitch
- Promoting a business—pottery-making lessons

CHAPTER 12

- IFA electronics show
- A hyperlapse tour

Preface

This book is designed to help you quickly master the techniques for making great short-form video content with your smartphone.

The chapters are organized around commonly used story themes and include mini-tutorials that introduce the key principles of filmmaking.

Each chapter includes online video examples of each story form and takes you behind the lens where you will learn:

- The key elements for each story form
- Pre-production planning
- Storyboarding
- How to film the shots
- How to edit the footage into a story
- The ethics and challenges
- How to use mobile video apps

By the time you complete the included practice filming, exercises, you will be familiar with the building blocks and processes for planning, filming, and editing a wide range of video stories with a smartphone.

The chapter lesson videos discussed in each chapter were filmed in 10 countries and are available to readers at www.smartfilmbook.com.

You will learn how to:

- Film and edit broadcast-quality video
- Quickly produce video stories for social media
- Select the right apps and gear
- Produce a portfolio of visual stories
- Make high-quality video interviews
- Write and record a great script
- Broadcast a live video report

This book is for anybody who wants to make video stories with a smartphone. This includes:

- Classroom teachers, media instructors, and communications students who are looking for a project approach to learn the best practices and behaviors for social video.
- Journalists who need to produce short-form video for social media platforms.
- Social media professionals who want to make video content with a smartphone.

NON-FICTION STORYTELLING

The story examples in this book flow from my experience as a journalist and journalism professor. I produce non-fiction videos, and the ethics and challenges of genuine, fact-based visual storytelling are ingrained into these examples.

Acknowledgments

I would like to thank the many journalists and media students to whom I have had the privilege to teach this material in my travels as a visiting professor. The universities where I teach and the many organizations that have invited me to lecture and produce workshops have provided me with the raw material for this book, and have enriched my own journey as a storyteller. I would like to thank you all, and hope that I will be able to return once again to share new filmmaking adventures.

My wife Jördis deserves special recognition because, in many instances throughout the making of this book, she has served as a teaching assistant, filmmaking partner, travel leader, illustrator, photographer, and documentarian. She drew the information graphics that are sprinkled across the chapters. Without her gracious assistance and indomitable spirit, this book could not have been made.

CHAPTER 1

Introduction

This chapter introduces the fundamentals for setting up your smartphone for filming. It includes online videos to orient you to the types of stories you can produce with a mobile phone.

Online Videos

- A big electronics show in Berlin

Quick Start Guide

- Manual control
- Filmic Pro
- Camera usage
- Shot sizes

Exercise

- Film like a pro

Figure 1.1 This online multimedia report that shows several video story forms that can be produced by a single person covering an event.

ONLINE VIDEOS

Watch the videos for this chapter at www.SmartFilmBook.com.

In this opening chapter I want to give you a sense of the many types of video storytelling you can make with a smartphone. Please view the multimedia report that I made from a large consumer electronics show that takes place every year in Berlin.

To see it, log into the online classroom using the link above to witness all of the social video content that was produced by one reporter carrying one iPhone.

ONLINE EXAMPLE 1.1

A Big Electronics Show in Berlin

Many of these micro stories were produced and posted to social media channels in almost real time. I compiled them all into this multimedia package to explain how I approached the scene.

In the package you will see many of the story forms that I teach in the book chapters.

This report includes examples of walkthroughs, interviews, and fast facts videos, and introduces some of the cinematic filming and editing techniques that you will learn.

This book is designed to teach you fundamentals for visual storytelling so that whatever camera you have with you, you will know how to use it find, capture, edit, and share your stories.

Along the way you will learn about the apps and gear that can provide professional results.

There are so many fascinating dimensions to learning the art of filmmaking, and it is my pleasure to get you started right away.

You can choose any chapter topic that interests you and begin to build a foundation of filmmaking knowledge that will stay with you, no matter what gear you use to make it.

Let me first introduce to you the filming fundamentals that you can use right away.

Figure 1.2 Journalists learn to film with smartphones at a film walk led by the author at the International Journalism Festival in Perugia, Italy.

Figure 1.3 On iOS devices, you manage the default camera settings with the Settings app. In the Photos & Camera pane you can set the resolution and frame rate for the video camera.

QUICK START GUIDE

This technical checklist will begin to transform your smartphone into a pro video camera:

- Enter airplane mode
- Disable notifications
- Disable portrait lock
- Check the battery power
- Clear memory storage
- Test your mic and audio levels
- Observe the lighting (quality and direction)

Why Disable Airplane Mode?

Every smartphone has a cell phone radio inside and it needs to be disabled because it can cause audio interference. Cell phones make frequent contact with nearby cell towers and these signals are sometimes recorded when filming. Be aware that this audio interference can also happen when you are livestreaming video. Mobile journalists usually carry portable WIFI connections with them when livestreaming to prevent this from happening.

On-screen notifications are not only a visual distraction when filming, they may actually halt your camera app in the middle of recording a scene.

Settings for Video

Figure 1.4 Maximize your device's memory before starting any important film project. Back up your photos and videos to an external drive before deleting them from your device.

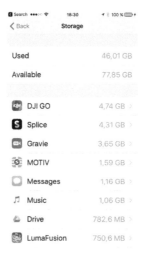

Figure 1.5 Apps can take a lot of memory, too. Watch out for those video editing apps that make copies of the video clips.

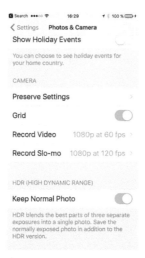

Figure 1.6 Activate the framing grid.

These are the default settings I use to capture high-quality video with my iPhone.

1080p is high-quality HD video and 60 frames per second helps capture smoother video. I also want to capture slow-motion video clips at the highest quality.

Slow-motion is a capture mode that that records more frames per second. For example, 120 frames per second video can be played back at a standard 30 frames per second in a video editor, and all the motion will appear four times slower and very fluid and smooth.

30 Frames per Second and 25 Frames per Second

30 frames per second is the default frame rate for all smartphones. It is based on the TV standard for North America. In Europe and almost everywhere else 25 frames per second is the TV standard. This frequency mismatch can cause light-flickering issues to be visible in video filmed under artificial light.

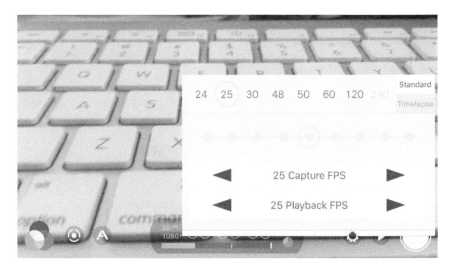

Figure 1.7 To correct for light flicker, you can use a pro video camera app like Filmic Pro to capture footage at 25 frames per second.

Manual Control

The smartphone you have in your pocket is an amazing video production machine.

The key to capturing pro footage is to escape out of the fully auto mode and learn how to film in fully manual mode.

Here are some tips to help you unlock that power.

With the built-in video camera app, you can get a degree of manual control by locking focus and exposure. The way this works on many phones is by disabling the AF (autofocus) and AE (auto exposure) controls.

Figure 1.8 With the iPhone camera app, just tap and hold on the screen until the AE/AF LOCK bar appears on screen.

The focus is now locked, but you can still adjust the exposure by sliding the icon of the sun up and down to make the exposure lighter or darker.

If the focus is not correct, just tap once to reset the camera to auto mode, and tap and hold on the area you want to focus on.

To gain more reliable and independent control over focus and exposure I like to use a pro camera app like Filmic Pro.

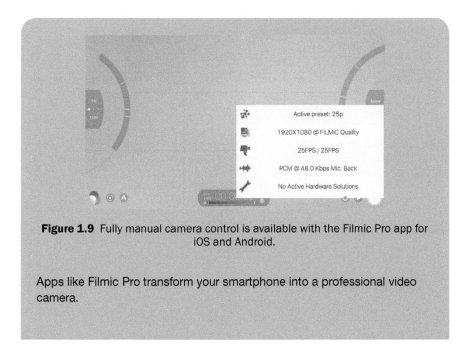

Figure 1.9 Fully manual camera control is available with the Filmic Pro app for iOS and Android.

Apps like Filmic Pro transform your smartphone into a professional video camera.

This pro video camera app provides you with manual control over exposure, focus, resolution, and frame rate. It also features slider controls that let you fine-tune exposure and focus, and the on-screen display provides other useful information about what your camera is seeing.

Practice first with the exposure setting to make sure your shots are lit well, and notice how consistent your video clips are when the light levels aren't being automatically adjusted by the camera.

Once you are comfortable with this, move on to the focus control and learn how to lock focus on what you want viewers to look at.

Shooting in manual takes some practice, so make several short test clips until you get the hang of it.

Figure 1.10 Reporters at TVN broadcasting in Warsaw, Poland, attach an Osmo mobile gimbal to their smartphones to record smoother handheld shots. The Filmic Pro app syncs to the Osmo mobile to provide hand grip controls for activating the record button, controlling focus and more.

Camera Usage

The next step is to use a reliable camera technique for filming your shots.

Horizontal Orientation

Film in landscape mode, unless specifically making a story form that features vertical framing.

Stabilization

Mount your camera to a tripod, a gimbal, or to anything that is not moving in order to capture smooth video.

Enable IOS (image optical stabilization) if your phone offers the feature.

Sneaker Zoom

No zooming. The "zoom" on most smartphones is actually cropping. To film various shot sizes you will need to move your feet.

Film in 10-Second Clips

Filmmaking is the art of connecting shots together to tell stories. Most shots in a typical video or film only appear on screen for a few seconds. Filming your clips for a maximum of 10 seconds helps you easily find those shots later when you are editing your video.

Shot Sizes

Filming a subject with different shot sizes provides your video story with more visual variety and interest.

A shot size merely describes the amount of content seen. Wide, medium, and close-up are the basic shots, and there are many variations that can be made from these.

Below are three shots from a story I made about a street artist in Berlin.

Figure 1.11 This wide shot establishes the location, the artist, tourists, and an activity.

Figure 1.12 This medium shot is filmed from an overhead angle to show the art being made.

Figure 1.13 The close-up shot filmed a low angle lets the viewer enjoy the many colorful details.

EXERCISE

Practice filming a few 10-second clips in manual mode using the basic shot sizes of wide, medium, and close.

Great!

You have completed your first filmmaking exercise and now have some sample clips on your camera roll that you can use when learning how to edit videos.

CHAPTER 2

A Portrait

Introduce a person with a video sequence.

Key Concepts

- Filming with a shot pattern
- Sequences
- Line of action
- The 180 degree rule
- Cutting on the action
- Framing vertical video
- Camera motion
- Slo-motion filming
- Text overlays

Online Videos

- Video profile in Singapore
- Vertical video in Paris
- Olya in Lviv

App Tutorial

- Editing social video

Exercise

- Film a portrait sequence using a shot pattern

Figure 2.1 Portrait scenes are used to introduce a character to a viewer in a way that reveals elements of their personality.

ONLINE VIDEOS

Watch the videos for this chapter at www.SmartFilmBook.com.

Goal

In this chapter you will learn how to work with subjects on camera.

Challenges

Putting subjects at ease and earning their trust to deliver a good on-camera performance is critical for capturing authentic film portraits.

We begin filming subjects using a typical shot pattern to work through the process of making them more comfortable in front of the lens.

Figure 2.2

ONLINE EXAMPLE 2.1

Video Profile in Singapore

This video is a brief character sketch that introduces a woman walking among her co-workers.

Building Blocks

I use a walking shot pattern in this portrait sequence.

The shots include:

- Tracking
- Feet
- Reverse tracking
- POV
- Face

Figure 2.3 TRACKING—The subject walks and the camera follows her at the same pace. I used a medium shot size for the framing. This is a variation of an OTS or "over-the-shoulder" shot, which is commonly used when filming sequences of people. Note that with a standard OTS shot, the camera does not move.

Figure 2.4 FEET—A close-up shot of the ground shows the subject's shoes as she continues walking.

Figure 2.5 REVERSE TRACKING—The subject walks forward and the camera operator walks backwards while maintaining the same distance from the subject's face.

Figure 2.6 A POV is a point-of-view shot, and it shows what the scene looks like from the subject's perspective. This unique perspective is a type of "neutral shot" because the subject is not seen in the frame. Neutral shots are very useful when editing clips together in a video because they help solve continuity and timing problems in the flow of images.

Figure 2.7 FACE—In this face shot the subject makes a head turn that is filmed in slow motion. This shot provides a satisfying end to the sequence. When filming the face shot, ask your subject not to talk. Having a non-talking face shot allows you to use that shot later with a soundbite of the person talking and it looks and sounds correct.

Variations

Be sure to film at least two variations for each shot. For example, change the angle, or the shot size.

Power Tips

- Remember to film each shot of the pattern for only 10 seconds.
- Do not use the zoom controls of your camera. Use your feet (sneaker zoom!) and move the camera closer.
- Don't forget to frame each shot as steadily as you can. Use a gimbal if possible and lock focus and exposure.
- Stay steady and let the subject enter and leave your frame.

Location

On a rooftop in Singapore.

Lighting

Filtered sunlight.

Apps

Native video camera app in "Slo-mo" video mode. I set mine to record at 240 frames per second.

Setups

One of the things you have to do before filming a walking portrait is to establish a "line of action" for your subject.

Point out two distinct marks on the ground where you want the subject to begin and end walking for each film take.

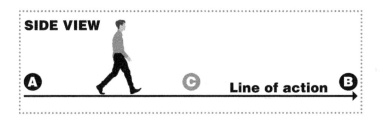

Figure 2.8 To make the close-up shot of the feet in the lesson film, the camera was located close to the ground at position C and the subject walked from A to B.

It may seem basic, but if you don't show people where to stop, they will just keep on walking and walking because they think you need more time for the filming (and also because they are not looking back to see you waving at them to stop!).

I indicate three positions for my subject: A, B, and C.

The subject will always start at the A mark and stop at the B mark. They are instructed to reset to the A mark after they hear the director yell "Cut."

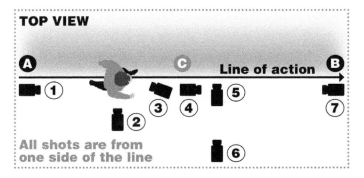

Figure 2.9

Here are seven typical camera positions for filming a walking sequence:

1. Over-the-shoulder. Variations: Film from a fixed position as well as a tracking shot. A tracking shot involves the camera following the subject.
2. Profile. Variations: Film different shot sizes from a fixed position as well as a camera trucking motion shot. A trucking shot involves the camera moving in the same direction and parallel to the subject.
3. Face. Film from a fixed position as well as a reverse-tracking shot. Take care when walking backwards and rehearse this shot with your subject to get a good take.
4. POV. The camera operator films at the eye level of where the subject has been walking. Your subject is not needed or shown in this shot.
5. Feet. Film a close-up of the ground with your subject's feet wiping past the lens.
6. Establishing and neutral shots. Show a wider view as well as film details of the environment without your subject to provide more editing choices later on.
7. A variation of the face shot with the camera much farther away from the subject.

To maintain the illusion of continuity, the subject must walk the same way each time and the background must also be the same. If the background changes, you will need to reshoot your pattern.

I explain to my subject that for some shots the camera operator may stop at mark C, but that they need to ignore the camera and the distractions to continue walking past until they reach mark B.

It is helpful to rehearse this choreography before filming.

This kind of dance with the camera is especially helpful when filming reverse tracking shots, because having the subject walk past the camera (and thus leaving the frame) provides a natural cut point in the footage where I can switch to show another shot in the sequence.

Restricting all of your camera positions to one side of the line strengthens the continuity of the sequence.

The Line of Vision

This is also known as the 180 degree rule and it applies to filming sporting matches and filming dialogue scenes with actors.

The reason that you do not want to cross the line in these situations is that you don't want the teams to be switching sides when you cut between live video shots of a soccer match. Similarly you don't want characters who are engaged in an exchange of dialogue to suddenly switch sides from screen right to screen left or vice versa.

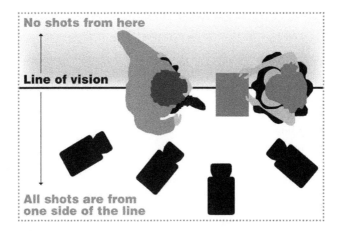

Figure 2.10 A typical TV show is filmed with one camera. Actors repeat their lines and the camera is moved to several different shot locations between takes to collect a variety of different angles. Over-the-shoulder shots are a staple of this type of filmmaking. The continuity of the movement and moment is maintained when the actors are able to repeat their performance with each take with the same emotion and gestures.

Editing the Video

You can edit a portrait sequence with any video-editing app that allows you to trim and order clips on a timeline. iMovie or Splice work just fine for this.

"Cutting on the action" is a polishing step that you can practice to gain deeper skills and insights as a video producer. Look at the walking shots closely (and in particular the close-up of the shoes) and trim your clips so that when you cut to the next shot the same foot is landing and at the same pace. This fine-tuning is really important to maintain continuity in the sequence.

Note that I added in a couple of still frames of her co-workers playing in the same space where we were filming. This provides some visual variety and also accounts for the passage of time to set up the final shot.

EXERCISE

Make a Sequence With a Shot Pattern

A portrait feature is an excellent way to practice filming in sequences.

I want you to "film a friend" to get familiar with this important skill. Sequences are a series of video clips that form a visual sentence when placed one after another.

Some shots work like nouns and others as verbs and conjunctions to form a grammatical statement—a visual statement that can be subconsciously understood by your audience.

What story questions can we answer for a viewer about our friend?

- Who is this person?
- How does that person get to their job?
- Where is that located?
- Who else is going that way?
- What happens when they are there?
- How exactly do they do their tasks?
- What does it look like from their point of view?
- How do others react when they see them doing it?
- What else is happening while they are doing it?
- How has the world changed now that they have done it?

These questions are answered with the camera. The resulting clips provide you with the visual nouns, verbs, modifiers, and conjunctions you need to tell their story in a sequence.

Film a Friend

For this exercise I can imagine that your friend drives into the city from the suburbs. (You can adapt this scenario to your situation.)

Here is how to develop a shot list for that activity.

You begin by recording a shot of them at their home. This kind of shot is called an *establishing shot* because it establishes a character and an activity.

You could then film their hand turning the knob on the front door as they leave the house. This kind of shot is a close-up shot shows your subject's *hands*.

The next shot you could film is an *over-the-shoulder* shot as your friend drives off. You can film this view from the back seat, for example.

Along the journey you might stop somewhere and film a *creative* shot showing other drivers and cars joining the commute. Maybe you record a time-lapse clip from a low angle with cars racing past.

When your friend looks back at the cars behind them, he or she will peek into the windshield mirror. This repetitive action allows you to get a close-up shot of your friend's *face*. In this case, his or her eyes will be framed in the mirror. This is a pretty cool shot to try for!

Just be sure that safety is observed and discuss this in advance with your friend to be sure.

The next shot can be a *neutral* shot like a *point-of-view* (POV) shot. A POV is simply a shot in which your camera records what your subject's eyes are looking at. So just turn around and film the cars traveling behind the one that you are in.

Congratulations, you have just filmed six shots that can be easily assembled into a visual sequence.

The Six-Shot Pattern

- Establishing
- Neutral
- Face
- Hands
- Creative
- OTS—over-the-shoulder

Your Turn

Film each shot of your friend for between 8 and 10 seconds.

It is important to film a couple of variations of each shot type. For example, shoot the same type of shot (creative, hands, establishing, etc.), but deliberately change the shot size (medium, close, or wide) and angle (high, low, neutral).

At the end of filming you will have around 15 clips in your photo library to edit a sequence with. For the soundtrack you can use narration, or a soundbite of your friend speaking, the ambient sounds of traffic, or just music.

» Visit the "Edit Video in iMovie" mini-tutorial in Chapter 3 for some quick video editing tips.

Bottom Line

Sequences are a filmmaker's best friend. They provide you with the creative power to introduce subjects into your film, transport them from one location to another and provide your viewers with visual answers to story questions.

A Brief History of Shot Patterns

Shot patterns have been used since the dawn of filmmaking.

Figure 2.11 Kodak published this Cine Photoguide in 1952 when the first hobby filmmakers were making home movies. (Photo courtesy of Prof. Michael Stoll.)

The Kodak Movie Organizer wheel introduced the concept of filming with shot patterns to a new generation of filmmakers who were using small film cameras.

Figure 2.12

ONLINE EXAMPLE 2.2

Vertical Video in Paris

This video shows a variation of the walking portrait sequence. It was produced for mobile phone viewers who may be more familiar with Snapchat videos.

Building Blocks

Richard is a co-instructor for my advanced filmmaking class at the EFJ School in Paris. We teach the journalism students how to build pilot episodes and rapidly prototype film projects using experimental techniques. I drafted him as a film model during one of our seminars with graduate students to develop a style for a vertical video walking shot sequence.

One of the student teams needed some guidance building a short-form video story format around tasty lunch spots in Paris. Their video pilot will feature culinary critiques. The shot pattern shown in the lesson film demonstrates one way to build a style for introducing food critics in those videos.

Each day a different critic would provide a lunch spot recommendation, so establishing a signature visual style for the series helps build a memorable brand and familiar expectation in the viewer's mind.

Location

Levallois-Perret, Paris.

Lighting

Available.

Props

We filmed in the courtyard of the school, where I had spied a cool ladder attached to a wall.

Storyboard

The main concept in filming vertical video is to have as little motion as possible.

Notice that the camera is not moving in this shot sequence, only Richard does.

Also, the sequence opens up in slow motion, again to limit the amount of motion and to build a little mystery as to who today's lunch critic will be.

The second shot is the magic shot in the sequence. Notice that the shot size switches from wide to medium, and that we let Richard brush right past the camera quite closely. We rehearsed this and made a couple of takes to get it right.

In the next shot, the action of the right foot swinging forward exactly matches the pace Richard established while walking past the camera. Note that the over-the-shoulder shown here is a steady shot that holds until Richard exits through the door.

This leaves the viewer with a shot frame that is "content neutral"—it is neutral because Richard is no longer visible.

This lets me bring in the last shot of Richard's face: a slo-mo shot that combines with a series of text overlays that give his comments on the lunch spot.

Apps

Filmic Pro, Splice video editor, and Gravie text editor.

CAMERA: I made a preset in Filmic Pro that would allow me to film at 1080p resolution and at 240 frames per second in 9:16 aspect ratio. 9:16 is full-frame vertical.

Figure 2.13 EDITING: I edited the sequence with Splice video editor, paying close attention to the details of matching his action. I exported the video to my camera roll and opened it up with Gravie text editor where I added text overlays at the correct moments in time. I then exported the project out to the camera roll.

Figure 2.14 The colored horizontal stripes seen in Gravie text editor indicate the editable text overlays.

Figure 2.15

ONLINE EXAMPLE 2.3

Olya in Lviv

A video profile of a woman who works in a street kiosk.

Building Blocks

I filmed this street portrait in Lviv while leading a film walk workshop. Film walks (also known as "photo safaris," or "photography immersion" workshops) are an opportunity for my students to venture out to discover, capture, and edit an original, unscripted film scene with a smartphone.
» Learn more: www.filmwalks.com.

Pre-production Planning

When I am teaching professional reporters, I challenge them to focus on reaching out to real people that they encounter on the film walk and practice making a video portrait of them. I practice what I preach, so Olya is a young woman I approached in the old town of Lviv. The city center is lined with kiosks like the one where she works, and this brief profile is a vignette that helps tell a larger story of city life. Filming strangers on camera can be a real challenge when you only have 60 minutes to wander around and find a good subject and film the portrait shot pattern.

Ethics

Every shot for this portrait (except for the face shot) was captured as events unfolded. There was no direction from me and I did not ask the people in the scene to repeat an action. Photojournalists are trained not to manipulate or set up people being filmed in a documentary setting.

Authenticity is a reporter's currency. This photojournalism ethic demands the reporter to be laser-focused on getting the shots they need. With practice, the instincts for anticipating actions and getting you and your camera in position to film something important are born. Do not leave the scene until you have filmed as many variations as possible. Especially those neutral shots! Opening and closing shots establish the location and the activity that is taking place. They were filmed before and after the portrait filming of Olya.

Location

Lviv, Ukraine.

Lighting

Diffuse, early morning light.

How This Was Filmed

When I first approached Olya at her kiosk, I bought a coffee and made some small talk with the help of my translator. She was just opening up her shop, so I asked her if it was OK if I filmed her doing her job. I said that I thought her job looked interesting and that I would like to make a portrait. She agreed and I filmed the slo-mo face shot of her outside her kiosk. She may have thought I was just snapping a still photo because it often looks like that when filming in slo-mo mode. This allowed me to capture a few seconds of her smile.

I then asked her to simply ignore me for the next few minutes as I continue to film additional shots of her working and serving customers.

Editing the Video

At the end of the film walk I met with the students at a café and I edited this scene with the Quick video editor app to demonstrate how to assemble the sequence, trim and order clips, and also add text overlays. We posted our portrait videos to social media before most other conference participants had eaten breakfast!

EDITING SOCIAL VIDEO

When sharing video clips on social media platforms and chat apps it can be handy to use a simple app that makes easy work of the editing.

Quik Video Editor

If you have a mix of photos and short video clips, the Quik Video app allows you to edit them together into a micro film that is perfect for Instagram sharing.

You can crop, trim, reorder, and title clips with text.

Once you have your story sequence set, toggle between the different presets in the app to preview different animation and editing styles.

Figure 2.16 Some of the editing preset styles are strange, some are slick, all are very creative. The **lapse** preset is a very neutral choice and a good one to audition first if you are using animated text subtitles.

When you find one you like, you can tweak the style settings, and of course you can go back in and edit the text and images you have in your sequence.

You can produce some amazing short-form video with Quik.

CHAPTER 3

Explainer

Demonstrate a process, reveal something new, or provide details about an issue.

Key Concepts

- Voice-over narration
- Timeliness
- Microphone usage
- Framing
- Stability

Online Videos

- Bild—No news photos in the newspaper?
- Unboxing a Beastgrip Pro and Moondog Labs lens

App Tutorials

- Creating social video with Twitter
- Getting started with iMovie

Exercise

- Film an explainer video

Figure 3.1

ONLINE VIDEOS

Watch the videos for this chapter at www.SmartFilmBook.com.

Goal

At the end of an explainer video a viewer should feel satisfied that they've been shown something fresh and now understand better what they have been looking at in a visual sequence.

Challenges

The two lesson video examples in this chapter use voice narration and a POV camera shot-framing angle.

One of the challenges with recording spoken word audio is to find a continuous train of thought that leads a viewer through the visual narrative.

One of the ways to overcome that challenge is to craft the words into a script that can be spoken while filming the scenes. Another technique is to record short verbal statements while filming short clips with the camera.

Figure 3.2 Bild is a German newspaper that decided to print a special edition with no news photographs to make a statement to their readers.

ONLINE EXAMPLE 3.1

Bild—No News Photos in the Newspaper?

This explainer video shows a very unusual newspaper event.

Building Blocks

For this explainer video I wanted to show as many pages of the newspaper as I could in an economy of time.

Pre-production Planning

This was a very fast turnaround video. It was filmed, edited, and posted within about 15 minutes.

Timeliness was one of the key ingredients in its viral success. Because newspapers only come out once a day and because I was in Berlin, I was able to send a branded video to my audience in almost real time and scoop all other media outlets.

The pre-production was fairly simple. I wanted to record one statement while filming a newspaper page or page turn.

I jotted down a few keywords that would remind me of the most important elements that I wanted to communicate.

Location

The floor of my flat where window light would illuminate the large newspaper pages.

Setups

I attached a lapel mic to the smartphone and filmed hand-held using the Twitter app.

Compose a new tweet, select the photo icon, and then tap on the video camera icon to enter the video camera and editor pane.

Figure 3.3 When filming each clip you need to tap and hold the red video camera icon. Release when you have spoken your short narration.

Props

Bild is a full-size broadsheet newspaper. When you open a double-page spread you realize just how big German newspapers are. It is so huge that I had to practice my moves once or twice to be able to coordinate keeping one hand on the newspaper and the other hand on the camera.

Filming the Shots

You can use any camera app to record an explainer video, just start and stop the recording for each statement you want to make and the visuals you want to show.

To emphasize the visual impact, I framed my shots with a medium close-up shot size so that the viewer would never see the entire newspaper in any one shot. In this case the discipline in using only medium close-up shots establishes visual tension and holds a viewer's interest.

Figure 3.4 You can delete, re-record, and reorder the clips in the Twitter app, but you cannot trim them.

Figure 3.5 I selected the Twitter app because of timeliness. I wanted one app where I could shoot, edit, and share a video to my social media audience—and Twitter is perfect for that.

Another App for Editing Video

You can also instead choose to edit an explainer video with a basic video editor like the iMovie app.

Figure 3.6

EDIT VIDEO IN iMOVIE

1. The clips from your filming project are in your camera roll (Photos app). We will use the iMovie app to edit the best of these shots together into a sequence.
2. Download and install the iMovie app.

Figure 3.7

3. Create a new "Movie" project.

Figure 3.8

4. Tap on the Video tab in the Media pane to preview your clips.
5. Identify a clip to start your sequence. Hint: It often helps to choose the most visually interesting one. If you don't have a strong opening shot, then choose an establishing shot.
6. Use the left and right yellow handles on the clip to trim it to the best 3 seconds. Then tap the check mark and "Create Movie" to add the clip to the timeline.

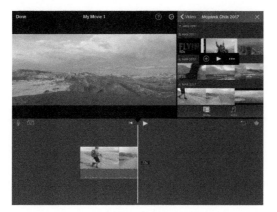

Figure 3.9

7. Tap on the Videos pane to select, trim, and add the next clip to your sequence. Your goal is to find four shots of 3 seconds each that visually flow seamlessly from one to the next. Look for connections between the shots: an object, person, a hand, a motion, and etc.
8. Tap "Done" in the top left corner and rename your project.

Figure 3.10

9. Tap the share icon (square with an arrow pointing up).
10. Tap "Save Video" to export your video to the camera roll.

Figure 3.11

Variations

You can choose to use text overlays instead of voice-over narration. This might give you more control for the text narrative and it would of course work for social media platforms where the audio may be muted.

Using text overlays would not have been a good choice for this Bild report, because the newspaper already has so much large text that adding subtitles would create a visual conflict for the viewer.
» You can take a deeper dive into script writing and recording broadcast-quality voice-over narration with the step-by-step video tutorials in the Mobile Journalism Certificate Course at the Smart Film School.

Exercise

Look around where you are right now and select an object that seems interesting enough for you to say three or four things about. On an index card, jot down a few keywords to remind yourself of the thoughts that you want to express when filming this object.

Now open up a camera app and look for a good location where the lighting is even and there are no distracting people talking or loud noises.

Record each of your thoughts while framing the object. Maybe for one shot, the object can be in your hand. For another shot it can be on the desk. Maybe you change to an overhead view and also film an extreme close-up shot to provide some visual variety.

Look again at that first frame of the Bild video example to see how I used an extreme close-up shot to open the video.

Figure 3.12 Unboxing videos are very popular on YouTube, and it's a straightforward form of video production.

ONLINE EXAMPLE 3.2

Unboxing a Beastgrip Pro and Moondog Labs Lens

Building Blocks

The key to making unboxing videos is to have something worth watching be opened up. New camera gear is a subject that is always going to find an audience online.

Pre-production Planning

Unboxing videos can look deceptively simple and they can be done quickly.

There are just a few key things to keep in mind.

To get best results, you'll want to use a tripod, a very simple table, consistent lighting, and a quiet space.

Location

I received this camera gear on a trip to the US and filmed the video in the kitchen of my brother's house.

Setups

I always travel with a small tripod that attaches to my smartphone and I was able to put this on the table and frame my shot to include all of the items that would be unboxed.

I positioned myself behind the tripod and made sure my hands could comfortably open up the boxes while filming was happening.

I attached a small lapel mic to the smartphone and clipped the capsule to my shirt. » You can see examples of microphones (and prices for different budgets) at the video gear page at www.GearTest.video.

Figure 3.13 The Sennheiser ClipMic Digital is a small clip-on microphone with a digital interface that provides broadcast quality audio to an iOS device.

Props

I like to film unboxing scenes in one take. I don't want to have to do extensive editing afterwards. I want to record a clean take so that all I have to do is trim the clip and add my branding and text overlays that will help improve the visual storytelling.

To make this possible, I'll take a small razor blade and cut open any taped elements of the boxes prior to filming. This makes it a lot easier and natural for the performer to proceed with a smooth unboxing event.

Voice-over Preparation

It can help to rehearse the unboxing sequence and make some mental notes of each phase to guide you when filming.

Apps

I used the Filmic Pro video camera app to record this unboxing sequence at the highest quality. Filming in manual mode allowed me to get stable focus and a consistent exposure. I then edited the video using the Splice app (or I could have just as easily used iMovie or LumaFusion).

Editing the Video

After I had recorded a good take, I stopped filming and confirmed that the clip was saved to the photo library. I then opened up the Splice video editor app and imported that clip into the timeline.

I added the visual branding (the animation sequence of the Smart Film School logo) as a clip from my library. These types of video assets are called "bumpers" and they are pre-made. In my case, I created this animation in Final Cut Pro and then transferred the short clip to my iPhone using Airdrop.

I keep my bumpers in a special library on my phone so that I can consistently brand videos that I make and share from the field.

CHAPTER 4

Fast Facts

Make a fact-driven visual report.

Key Concepts

- Short-form storytelling
- Photo editing
- Writing to pictures
- Organizing facts and figures
- Text animation
- Ethics for editing

Online Videos

- What is inside Egypt's pyramids?
- By the numbers
- BBC—An avalanche of ethics

App Tutorial

- Legend text editor (Basic)

Exercise

- Make a video from photos

Figure 4.1 A fast facts video is a no-nonsense, bare-bones, fact-driven visual report.

ONLINE VIDEOS

Watch the videos for this chapter at www.SmartFilmBook.com.

Goal

Produce a timely video that presents only the essential facts.

Challenges

Producing short-form video requires a clear and direct story focus.

This format will sharpen your skills in using pictures and words to tell memorable, non-fiction stories.

Figure 4.2

ONLINE EXAMPLE 4.1

What Is Inside Egypt's Pyramids?

This fast facts video was produced as a quick-turnaround response to refute false claims made by a candidate running for president.

Building Blocks

On November 5, 2015, USA Republican presidential hopeful Ben Carson said that he believes that the Egyptian pyramids were used to store grain. "My own personal theory is that Joseph built the pyramids to store grain," Carson said. His belief is not rooted in any facts.

I have visited several Egyptian pyramid tomb sites along the Nile and I can assure you that the pyramids are not hollow.

The small empty space inside is built for a tomb.

If a pharaoh were trying to store enough grain for his people to survive a famine, then he wouldn't design and build a stone pyramid for that task.

Pre-production Planning

I not only visited Egypt's pyramids over the last few years, I took lots of pictures.

To build this fast facts video story, I needed to gather the photos from my iPhoto library and find pictures from the Bent, Stepped, Khufu, and Red pyramid fields.

In my picture research I even found a picture showing me crawling inside the small entrance to Teti—one of the pyramids at the Saqqara pyramid complex.

This visual reporting supports the facts that archaeologists, historians, and scholars all agree on: that the pyramids are in fact, tombs.

The photos provide an authentic report about the pyramids based on my personal visual inspection. The fact that I appear in several of the photos further establishes the origin off the images as well as my credibility and authority.

And it shows—at human scale—the actual empty chamber sizes inside these massive stone monuments. A space completely unsuited for storing grain.

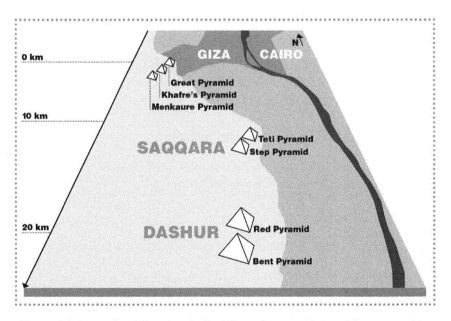

Figure 4.3 I toured and filmed at the Red, Bent, Saqqara, Teti, and Great pyramids. These sites are located in three different regions along the Nile.

Ethics

The ethics for this type of storytelling is direct and unambiguous. Anyone seeking elected office should be held to account for every falsehood they tell.

The U.S. Supreme Court has ruled that politicians are public figures who have "thrust themselves into the spotlight" and can expect to be questioned and criticized in public for making dubious statements.

A debunking video can also show a sense of humor. The basis for Carson's statement is so preposterous that it invites satire.

Preparation

I found the photos from my Egyptian expeditions and edited them into a slideshow.

I found selfies that I had made outside the Khufu pyramid in Giza, the Stepped pyramid at Saqqara, from inside the Teti pyramid, and outside the Red and Bent pyramids near Dashur.

Wordplay

The story title "A Grain of Truth" is a pun that ties strongly to the story and is loaded with irony. It is ironic because it references the old saying; "That behind every lie there is a grain of truth."

In this case, there is nothing credible about the candidate's statement about ancient kings storing "grain" in Egypt's pyramids.

Apps

I used the Quik video editor app on iOS to build the title cards and visual sequence.

Storyboard

I open with the title card, and then chose to show the photo showing me in front of the Great pyramids in Giza to pose the question: "What's inside Egypt's pyramids?"

The following scenes then visually answer that question with a repeating pattern of two frames: a title card animation followed by the photo with a text overlay.

- Title card: "Name of pyramid"
- Photo with text: "What you actually find there."

Editing the Video

Using the Quik video editor app, I added my photos, wrote the title cards, and then added the text overlays. Next, I auditioned several of the presets until I found one that matched the tone for this piece.

I exported the video as 1:1 square format and added my branding logo at the end using the Splice video editor app.

The Bottom Line

This clip was produced and posted in near real time and shared widely on social media within the news cycle for this item. Just be sure to double-check and triple-check your evidence before publishing a fast facts story.

Exercise

You can make a fast facts story using the Quik video editing app and five photographs.

Look around you right now. I bet you can tell a quick visual story about your favorite pet, person, or a treasured object using some fresh photos, and just the facts.

Figure 4.4

ONLINE EXAMPLE 4.2

By the Numbers

I love this little video because it shows that you can turn numbers into video and facts into memorable moments.

Building Blocks

This type of fast facts story alternates title cards of animated text with unusual shots filmed at a consumer electronics show in Berlin.

Pre-production Planning

I found the figures of the numbers of journalists, exhibitors, and participants attending the event from the consumer electronic show's official website.

I selected three shots from my filming that showed journalists, exhibitors, and participants.

Location

The IFS consumer electronics show is one of the largest in Europe and is held at a convention space called the Messe in Berlin.

Apps

To build this type of fast facts video I used two apps: Legend text editor and Quik video editor.

Editing the Video

I like to begin by creating the clips of my animated numbers.

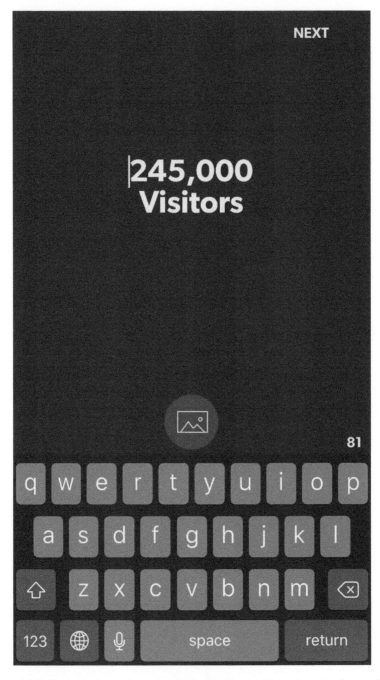

Figure 4.5 To create these I open up the Legend text editor app and enter my first number and text.

Figure 4.6 And then choose one of the 18 animation variations that the app builds and previews for me.

Figure 4.7 Tap to make your selection and then tap on the "... More" button.

Figure 4.8 Tap "Save Video" to copy the animated text as a video clip in your photo library.

Next I will open the Quik app and create a new project.

I then import the new animated text clips and the specific shots that I have previously identified as good matches for the numbers.

Note: To keep the style visually consistent, I quickly return to the Legend text app and create the first title card clip: "IFA BERLIN BY THE NUMBERS."

I then import this video into my project and position it as the first clip in the sequence.

I audition different music and editing presets in Quik until I'm happy with the tempo and the feeling of the video sequence.

Once I've exported the video clip to my photo library I can use it as part of my reporting.

In the first chapter online video example, you can see how I used this "by the numbers" clip in the multimedia story that I produced from the event.

Exercise

This is a great story form to practice. For your exercise I suggest to start with a topic that is familiar to you. You can choose the town where you live, for example, and collect figures that will help tell a visitor something unique about your community.

Then go out and film scenes that match the numbers you have found.

> **TIP**
> Focus on making shots of people.

Then, create your animated text using the Legend text app and assemble your video using the Quik video-editing app.

ONLINE EXAMPLE 4.3

BBC—An Avalanche of Ethics

German mountaineer Jost Kobusch captured the terrifying moment the Everest base camp was hit by an avalanche triggered by the Nepal earthquake.

The April 2015 Nepal earthquake (also known as the Gorkha earthquake) killed nearly 9,000 people and injured nearly 22,000.

Kobusch posted his footage to YouTube (www.youtube.com/watch?v=_JC_wIWUC2U).

NOTE: Kobusch can be heard cursing while filming the horror of an avalanche hitting the Everest base camp.

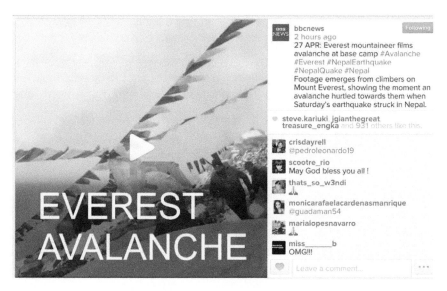

Figure 4.9 The BBC posted a video story card on their Instagram feed with Kobusch's footage. But they altered the audio track without providing an explanation.

The broadcaster has since removed the post, but you can see a replay of the video in the video example in the online section of this course.

They muted the eyewitness audio and added music and sound effects that were not present at the breaking news scene.

Figure 4.10 According to my Shazam app, the music presented with this breaking news clip is actually is a track titled "Antipathy," which is from a music library published by Gothic Storm Music.

The BBC posts video story cards on Instagram to reach millennials who may not normally get their breaking news reports. Their channel has more than 3.8 million followers.

I show these kinds of fast facts social video reports in my workshops as examples of how visual story cards can reach audiences who spend most of their time with their mobile phone.

They often work well in a streaming news environment.

I reached out to followers of my Twitter feed and was curious to learn:

At what point do you decide to alter the audio track of raw footage provided by an eyewitness/victim at a breaking news scene?

Figure 4.11

Cameron Robertson, a freelance video journalist with top credentials writes:

> Bleeping out the curse words is what CNN chose to do with their on-air presentation of this footage. Their package also provided context in the form of a 3D map that showed where the events took place.

Dan Graham, the CEO of Gothic Storm Music wrote to me.

> As library music, the BBC is free to use it as they see fit as part of their blanket license deal with MCPS but I have to admit, it seems like a pretty bad decision to me—it's designed for movie trailers not real tragedies.

I showed this to my friend, Marc Settle who is a Mojo trainer for the BBC.

> @robbmontgomery the original audio is basically the guy saying F★CK F★CK F★CK quite loudly, so something had to run in its place.

marc blank-settle (@MarcSettle), April 27, 2015

Of course, Marc is not the social media editor for the BBC and had no role in the editing the broadcaster makes for their Instagram channel.

So I next reached out to Mark Frankel, who is the new social media editor at the BBC in London and he writes.

> Yes this was before my tenure but, from memory and previous discussion with colleagues, there was no deliberate attempt to distort or mislead here.
>
> There was some initial concern about the swearing being audible on the video, hence the use of music. When senior colleagues became aware of this fact they clearly decided this was not appropriate/right and removed it.
>
> We take trust and transparency with audiences very seriously and will never set out to present a false impression of an original story.

I noticed that the BBC was pioneering a short-form slideshow video news format featuring smart visual editing, consistent subtitles, and branding, and I have shown many fine examples of their work at media conferences as examples of best practices.

It is important to also ask ethical question about treatment of breaking news because these feeds are reaching younger, mobile-centric audiences.

There was certainly a pattern of adding music to eyewitness video footage to BBC Instagram video reports at this time in 2015.

Another BBC Instagram post showing the damage in Kathmandu featured music mixed in with audio of people crying. The viewer is left wondering which audio is authentically from the scene.

Figure 4.12

If the music is added by editors in the post-production, were the sounds of crying also added?

A viewer can reasonably wonder which parts of the audio are real. If artificial music was added in post, were the sounds of crying also added? Probably not, but there is no explanation provided in the post.

How Did Others Present the Climber's Video Online?

Links to the videos for this chapter can be found at www.SmartFilmBook.com.

- CNN: Avalanche engulfing Everest base camp caught on video (see http://edition.cnn.com/2015/04/27/asia/nepal-earthquake-mount-everest/index.html).
- The Guardian published Kobusch's video without editing the audio track (see www.theguardian.com/world/2015/apr/27/nepal-earthquake-rescue-of-stranded-everest-climbers-begins).

CNN bleeped the curse words and The Guardian placed their "g" logo watermark on the video and only credits the source (Jost Kobusch) with a brief lower-third overlay mention and not in the article text itself. They do not link to, mention, or embed the original YouTube video.

The takeaway:

Does altering the audio track of raw footage provided by an eyewitness/ victim from a breaking news scene enhance or harm your credibility?

CHAPTER 5

Food

Produce a recipe video.

Key Concepts

- Studio filming
- Making a shot list
- Working with props
- Title cards
- Producing a postcard video for social media
- Animated text overlays

Online Videos

- Salad—shoot and edit a recipe
- Make a title card sequence
- Assemble a video postcard
- A studio approach to food shots

Mini Tutorial

- One meter closer

App Tutorials

- PicPlayPost
- Legend text (Advanced)

Exercise

- Produce a recipe video

Figure 5.1 I will show you how to make four types of food videos including the production steps that go into a studio film shoot.

ONLINE VIDEOS

Watch the videos for this chapter at www.SmartFilmBook.com.

Goal

At the end of this chapter, you will be able to film and edit a recipe video for sharing on social media.

The lessons in this chapter are progressive. Each example introduces new techniques. The exercises will provide you with material for the next lesson topic. This will help you gain confidence as you build your skills.

Challenges

Working with food presents some unique challenges because it often takes some time to set up certain shots. And sometimes this means you need to prepare the elements of the scene for a shot more than once so that you can get the best take and capture the food in the best possible quality. This is important if you're going to film a recipe video using the studio techniques that I am going to show you in this first example.

Figure 5.2

ONLINE EXAMPLE 5.1

Salad — Shoot and Edit a Recipe

This 15-second video was filmed as my wife and I prepared one of our favorite dishes—a fresh asparagus salad. White asparagus is a common treat in Germany and during "Spargel season" in April and May we make a wide variety of dishes that features this vegetable.

The video is composed of a sequence of close-up shots filmed with my iPhone. It was edited in the Storyo app.

Building Blocks

The purpose of sharing this recipe video was to show how simple the ingredients and how quick the food prep is for this tasty dish. There are only five ingredients plus a vinaigrette dressing.

As we were preparing the food, I was looking to make shots that communicated not only which ingredients were used, but also some of the activities that had taken place between frames. For example, peeling and chopping the asparagus and chopping the tomatoes.

Pre-production Planning

There was no planning as the filming was improvised. I was inspired by the colors and the simplicity of the steps.

Location

Kitchen counter.

Lighting

Because evening cooking is our nightly entertainment, I had upgraded the under-counter lighting with four strips of warm-color LED strips with diffusion covers. This affordable solution provides a blanket of warm, soft light, but only over the primary prep and cooktop areas.

Props

Transparent bowls, white bowls, and everyday china.

Ethics

I try to avoid the temptation to manipulate an environment that I am documenting with my camera. I am a #NoFilter photojournalist, so you won't find me often using consumer-oriented "filters" and presets to artificially color my work.

I feel it is always important to find the skills and the moments that allow me to frame a shot in a way that doesn't require any post-processing beyond setting highlights and shadows. That said, the Storyo app did desaturate the colors in the first frame of my video project, but I was OK with this in this case because that allowed the title text to be read more easily and because it also reveals the full color version in the next shot.

Preparation

I guess it is a habit with me and my wife to film our cooking adventures.

We carefully shop fresh ingredients and search out new recipes and kitchen tools and enjoy the prep work in the kitchen. That is not so say we are never messy, but attention to detail when making food together does elevate the cooking experience and also seems to invite the camera into the scene.

The key for many of these shots is to observe just how close the camera is to the food. This is done on purpose to frame out the messy stuff and also to pull the viewer into the details of the colors and textures. For example: the viewer does not to need to see the entire circle of a bowl in order to see that there is a bowl in the shot.

ONE METER CLOSER

What do you typically see when someone is taking of a photo of a friend?

They will often step backwards until they can see everything in a scene, including the subject's shoes.

That's a photo #fail.

You'll find success when you step IN with your camera and get closer to your subject.

This is especially important when filming food shots.

A smartphone camera has a wide-angle lens, so the only way to get true close-up details is to move in a lot closer than you would with a DSLR camera.

Apps

Camera: Native camera app in manual mode.

Editing: Storyo, Quik video editor, LP Converter.

Setups

Clean away the clutter so the focus is on the food. Use bowls and plates that highlight the food rather than stealing visual attention away.

Storyboard

This video is an example of "writing to pictures." The words came as a result of the photo edit and sequence. No advance planning was required in order to tell this photo story.

Takeaway

If you love to cook, then this approach can be an everyday treat for you as you document your home chef adventures without the burden of filming a "video." Why let film production get in the way of making the meal?

Editing the Video

The key to making a video like this is to always make a strict photo edit. You do this through role-play. As a photographer it can be hard to reduce your footage to just the essential shots that advance the story. I made 20 photos over the course of the cooking and, of course, I loved every one of them like a baby.

In a newsroom, the difficult task of cutting down a shoot is left to an impartial picture editor who evaluates the results and selects the best shots based on the storytelling potential from each moment, as well as the overall story arc.

So getting the edit down to just five shots is what makes the sequence powerful. No activity is duplicated so there is no wasted motion. It helps to make a significant pause between filming and editing to achieve this emotional distance from the effort put into filming. If there is no rush to post your recipe video, I would suggest that you sleep on it and in the morning do your ruthless photo edit.

The Storyo app itself is easy to use and will auto-fill out some text areas that you can then edit. And you can audition a few of the presets before you find the one that best suits your story.

Variations

Of course you don't have to use still photographs to make this type of quick recipe video. If you're filming with a late-model iPhone you can shoot instead with "live photos" mode. Live photos are actually low-frame-rate and lower-resolution video clips that record motion with a peculiar style.

Live photo video clips mimic the effect of the film-based Super 8 cameras that were a popular format for making home movies before handheld video camcorders entered the market in the 1980s. That is what gives them such a delightfully "retro" look and feel.

Make sure that live photos is enabled in the camera app by tapping the icon with three rings until it turns yellow.

Figure 5.3

For editing a video with live photos I like to use a video-editing app like Quik video editor. This app will natively import your live photos as videos without first having to convert them.

If you need to convert live photos to video clips for use in other video editing apps, you might try out LP Converter app—it is simple and effective.

Exercise

Now it's your turn. Think about a fun simple recipe you'd like to film. As you make the recipe (or your partner makes the food), capture 15 to 20 pictures along the way. And then put the camera down and go and enjoy your meal.

Wait for your photo edit until the next day. With a new frame of mind and a sharp focus, reduce your selections to the best five images that frame a story with a beginning, middle, and end.

The Bottom Line

Food is fun. We have to eat every day, so cooking and filming is a creative opportunity to work on your photography and visual storytelling skills.

Figure 5.4

ONLINE EXAMPLE 5.2

Make a Title Card Sequence

This video clip is about 6 seconds long and it was created to work as an introduction to a video recipe. Filmmakers call this type of clip a "title card" sequence and they are often used to bring a bit of a special introduction to video project.

Building Blocks

Title cards and animated text overlays are really important when you're making a video to be shared on social platforms. In this example, I have invited the viewer to watch a video recipe for making asparagus salad.

You can choose to have a title card that combines an image with text or you can choose to have plain text presented over a background color. White text titles on a black background are a common choice for many filmmakers.

Pre-production Planning

For this title card clip, I chose a close-up still image of the finished dish. I wanted the details to ring through but not compete too much with the animated text.

Apps

Once you have selected an image and thought of something to say it's time to open up the app you want to use to build the title card animation.

In this example I chose the Legend text app, because it's very simple to use and I don't have to know anything about making key frame animation.

Figure 5.5

Editing the Video

Step one is to open the Legend text app and select the small icon of the mountains in the middle of the screen.

This will open up your photos library where you can choose either a still image or video to be used in your project. If you choose a video you'll be prompted to trim it because the resulting title card sequence will be 6 seconds long.

Now you can simply write the words that you want to have animated over your image. You'll see that it will allow you to type up 100 characters. I would suggest thinking of three to five words that help draw the attention and attract interest in your recipe.

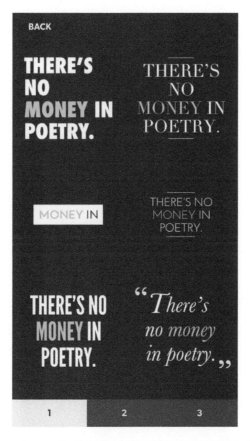

Figure 5.6 When you tap on the "next" button you'll be presented with 18 previews of your animation. The app will show you a preview of the first six on the first pane, the next six on the number two panes, and the final six on the number three pane.

At this point you can see if you need to adjust your text. For example you could tap on the back button and choose to put a return (or two) between thoughts if you would like to separate elements of the text.

Then you can click on the next button again to see it how the new formatting looks with your previews.

When you've selected one of the options you'll see a larger preview of the animation and at the bottom there will be a "more" button with "…" (an ellipsis).

When you tap on this, your video will be rendered and you will be prompted to save the clip to your camera roll.

Variations

When you're in the preview screen you may have noticed that there were a number of colored boxes with the letter "T" in them.

Figure 5.7 You can audition these various filters in real time by tapping on them. Don't forget to swipe right to see that there are many filter presets to choose from. Some of these are nice, others are kind of goofy.

Some of these will also alter the image that you may have added by applying a filter or blurring effect. You can't tweak these settings, unfortunately.

When you find one you like, tap on the "more" button and render that video and save it to your camera roll. At any point in this process, you can tap the "back" button and return to the screens where you edit your text, image, or formatting.

> **TIP**
>
> Title cards that employ a black background and white text represent the classical style for filmmaking.

Exercise

So now it's your turn. You can begin by opening up the Legend text app and playing with an existing image from your camera roll.

The Bottom Line

Using title card sequences can make your videos look more professional and inviting.

Figure 5.8

ONLINE EXAMPLE 5.3

Assemble a Video Postcard

In this example film we take elements from the previous lessons in this chapter and combine them into a video collage—a recipe "postcard" to share with chat apps and in social media posts.

Building Blocks

To make this collage, I used the title card sequence created in the previous lesson as well as the photo story with text overlays video clip shown in the earlier lesson.

I also added one of the still pictures from my photo shoot of the asparagus salad recipe.

Pre-production Planning

When you look at the sample video, I want you to pay attention to one key design element.

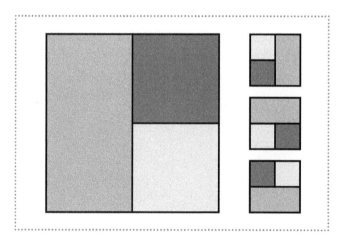

Figure 5.9 Power tip: When choosing a collage design, select a layout grid with only three image panes.

The reason for this choice of three panes is pretty straightforward.

I have already produced two square-shaped pieces of video and have a photo collection that includes at least one picture that works well with a vertical crop.

This simple three-pane design allows us to place these elements into a very pleasing arrangement that does not confuse the viewer.

This is important because when you first open a collage app, you'll find that the developers give you dozens of style choices and many of those can produce very cluttered postcard designs.

Preparation

Since this video requires you to have some already edited video material on your device, I recommend that you complete the two previous lessons in this chapter where I show you how to film and add a recipe picture story.

Apps

The app I like to use for making these postcard collages is one called PicPlayPost. It's got some great features that I don't find in some other collage-editing apps.

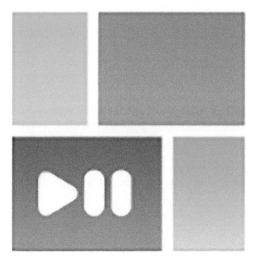

Figure 5.10

Editing the Video

The collage is a different piece of multimedia video. And it takes practice to get the best results.

Open the app and choose a square aspect ratio for the shape of your final collage.

Since we have created square video clips, selecting the 1:1 aspect ratio will create a square-shaped video collage while preserving the square video clips that we have previously built.

This first step is really important. Be sure to look for the small icon toward the bottom center of the screen that has some numbers like 16: 9 or 4:3 or 1:1 and make sure that you have got 1:1 selected.

Now select one of the designs that only have three panes. In my video example, you can see that I chose the one that has a vertical pane on the left and two squares panes on the right.

Tap on this design and you're presented with a full-size preview. Now you can tap on the plus buttons for each of the shapes to import your media. For each you can choose either a video or photo.

You should find that the square videos that you made from the Storyo and Legend text apps fit perfectly in the panes without cropping any of the text elements. If not, make sure you have selected the 1:1 aspect ratio for your project.

For the vertical pane, choose a photo that will work easily into that crop.

When you're happy with your collage, tap on the share button and save it to the camera roll.

Variations

When adding media to a pane, you may have noticed the "slideshow" option. Selecting this will prompt the app to build a short video clip from still photos into that pane.

And of course there are deeper editing functions that will allow you to determine the sequence of which videos will play first, or whether those video should replay in a loop.

Exercise

There are a lot of creative options with this app and with this story format. I recommend that you start by using the image you created from a previous lesson in this chapter and follow the steps that I'm showing above.

The Bottom Line

Once you get comfortable making your first video collage, you're well on your way to finding your own personal expression for creating and sharing postcard recipes.

The perfect **three-layer latte**

Figure 5.11

ONLINE EXAMPLE 5.4

A Studio Approach to Food Shots

Watch this video and pay attention to how many shots I used to show the process of making a latte. Making coffee is something we take for granted and this is actually how I make coffee for me and my wife every morning in our Berlin flat.

Because the coffee-making ritual is special and very visual, it's a good subject to explore with the camera.

Building Blocks

Recipe videos are really popular these days and many of these videos follow a familiar pattern where time-lapse sequences and speed-ramped portions of the scenes allow the process to be viewed in a short amount of time.

Text overlays provide critical details for the viewer, who is probably watching your film with the sound muted.

High-angle camera shots are typically used for filming recipe videos. The lighting must be consistent and soft and the background and stage deceptively simple.

In other words, not like the kitchen of the average person.

Each of these visual building blocks presents some challenges and opportunities for the filmmaker.

Pre-production Planning

For this type of video we will need to build a shot list, organize an improvised studio environment where the action will take place, and employ equipment that will stabilize the camera.

You will also need an off-camera staging area for food preparation and the organization of your props that you will use in the cooking sequence.

Of course, it helps if you have some stylish props to make your recipe video look attractive.

Location

You'll often get best results for shooting a recipe video if you can set up a temporary studio using a table where you can position the camera properly while still making the recipe and have consistent lighting during the course of your shoot. Taking care of these details at the start makes editing your video a lot easier and faster.

Lighting

I use two compact fluorescent studio lights with diffusion filters attached to make an evenly lit scene. The video studio lights I used in the coffee video are actually very low-budget "student-quality" lamps. At least that's the way they were described to me by the owner of the neighborhood photo store where I bought them.

In fact, there are a lot of university students who visit that store and those buyers are always on a tight budget.

A student-quality studio light is very different from a pro video light in some key areas: You can't adjust the color temperature between daylight and tungsten or change how strong the light power is.

The only way you can control the light is by moving it closer or farther away from the subject and by changing the angle. You can also cut down the amount of light by blocking some of the beam using a large foam core board clamped to a light stand.

For a simple food shoot with a small stage to light, a simple two-light approach works just fine. Just be sure to film after the sun sets or in a room where you can close off all outside light in order to maintain consistent lighting during your filming session. Paying attention to this detail will make your finished video look professional.

Props

The coffee video that I show in the example used very simple props, and the key for me was finding a transparent glass cup so that the viewer could clearly see the three layers in the latte.

This detail helps me make an attractive establishing shot (the first frame that the viewer sees) and also the final beauty shot. That single prop choice helps to create anticipation for what's to come and provides satisfaction for the viewer at the end of the process.

Ethics

Everyone wants their food to be as attractive as it can be and you may be tempted to take some short cuts to make it look more delicious.

I won't go into details about how you might do this, but I am aware of how food "stylists" often manipulate food items for television commercials and advertising photo shoots.

I just don't do it. And the reason for that probably comes from my editorial background working in newspapers like the Chicago Tribune as an art director for the food section.

As a journalist working in a professional newsroom we have a pact with our readers that we would never photograph phony food. We just would not take short cuts or use elements that were not in the recipe just to make a prettier picture.

That meant we had to work harder, we had to work smarter, and sometimes we had to work faster in order to get the pictures while the steam was coming off the food.

It's a point of pride if you can stand behind your work and feel good that what you're showing to your viewer is authentic, wholesome, and genuine. And isn't that the point of making great food?

Preparation

The storyboard is a shot list that describes everything you're going to film and what will be framed in camera.

This first step in your prep also describes the props, entrances, and exits of food and utensils, as well as any on-screen text that may be needed to make things clearer for the viewer.

I'm not going to kid you—it can take a while to really think through every step of your recipe using your "camera eye."

Look at that video again. There are more than a dozen shots strung together in that 30-second sequence. That's the real trick. This video is not just one long shot that was speeded up to make it play back faster. That would look pretty awful. The finished video is a reconstruction of the real process, filmed one step at a time.

I'll share with you the shot list for this video in just a moment, but there are a couple of other things you will also need to prepare before filming.

Apps

The apps I used make this video were Filmic Pro, Splice video editor, and Gravie text.

Figure 5.12

Filmic Pro gives you professional camera controls. For example, I can lock the focus and exposure so that all my shots will have the same lighting and a consistent quality.

I also used this app to film in 1:1 aspect ratio to capture a square-shaped video. I did this because I had intended to share this video on social media and the square shape works well for that purpose.

Figure 5.13

The Splice video editor is a very simple but effective timeline editor that allows you to trim and build a video sequence easily and simply.

Figure 5.14

Gravie Text is an app that allows you to add animated text overlays to a video once you've exported your video to your camera roll or photo gallery.

Setups

The gear I used for this shoot was pretty simple. I used a Shoulderpod grip to secure my phone to a tripod and I set up two fluorescent lights on either side of a small table.

To get the proportions right I opened up my camera app and started to see how items looked in the frame when I brought in different props like the milk froth or the hot water kettle.

I had to find a single position for the camera that I could use for the majority of the filming to allow these items to be clearly seen by the viewer. This involved making a few test shots to see how the reflections and the shadows were working.

I was trying to avoid visual distractions and having to move the camera for each shot.

This discipline maintains continuity for the final sequence.

After the initial shoot, I did move the tripod and camera closer and at different angles in order to record some detail shots of the kettle boiling and the application of the chocolate decoration.

And for my "beauty shot," I moved the camera back and shot a little bit wider and at a lower angle. It's in this shot that you can clearly see the background, so I went for something simple using some matte black paper taped to the wall.

I selected a flat, neutral color for the background so that my text overlays could be clearly read by the viewer.

Storyboard

The props:

- Milk frother
- Coffee mill
- French press
- Bowl
- Water kettle
- Cutting board
- Table
- Backdrop

The Scenes

Video opens with a beauty shot of finished coffee.

- TEXT: "The perfect three-layer latte"

MILK

- Pour milk into frother
- Milk container leaves frame
- TEXT: "Low-fat milk"
- TEXT: "Heat to 140 degrees F"

WATER

- Kettle slides in
- Flip switch
- Close-up: Water boiling

BEANS

- Pour beans into bowl
- Grinder slides in
- Pour beans into hopper
- Grinder slides out
- Hand grinding the beans

FROTH

- Milk frother slides in
- Lid drops in
- Frothing action
- Frother slides out

PRESS

- French press slides in
- TEXT: "French Press"
- Pour coffee grounds
- Water kettle wipes the frame as it moves toward press
- Pour boiling water
- TEXT: "Press coffee immediately"
- Close-up of lid dropping in
- Press grounds

POUR

- Empty glass on table
- Pour milk
- Frother jug exits
- French press enters and pours
- TEXT: "Pour slowly"

HAPPY ENDING

- Sprinkle chocolate

BEAUTY SHOT

- Branding logo
- TEXT: "The perfect three-layer latte"

I encourage you to really take the time and imagine all the shots you think you need to film, and then imagine your milk frother and your kettle as characters performing a play on a very small stage.

This visualization technique helped me to identify how I was going to move from scene to scene, and manage the entrances and exits of those characters from the stage.

Takeaway

Who knew it would take three hours to set up and film this video? That's the thing that can overwhelm you if you don't prepare in advance or allow enough time.

In reality it only takes me about five minutes to make this coffee every morning. I imagine that the filming might have gone a little faster if I had a helper, of course.

Editing the Video

Fortunately the editing did not take very long at all. And the reason for that is that I headed off potential problems with my edit by writing down all my shots and scenes as clearly as possible.

In the Splice video-editing app you can import all of the clips that you had filmed and begin to trim them and select the best takes in order to build your movie.

I like to work shot by shot when I begin my edit.

The first step is finding the best "in point" and the best "out point" for that clip. And then I'll move on to the next one. For a couple of my scenes I might have filmed a second or third take. I will quickly trim those as well and then find the best take.

And then I will simply delete the bad ones from the project.

Because I had filmed from a shot list, most of my shots should be in the correct order as I have imported them.

But if not, I will take that time to move a clip forward or backward on the timeline so that it makes sense for the viewer.

Also, if adding in one of my close-up shots helps a scene I will look for my close-ups that I filmed at the end and then train them and insert them into the sequence in the right position.

At this point I will often take a little break so that I can come back and look at my project with fresh eyes.

I will play the entire project from beginning to end and make some notes along the way of scenes that can be sped up or will need to be slowed down to give additional time for the text overlays to be read by a viewer.

And I refer to these notes as I adjust the speed for the clips. When I'm happy with the tempo and the continuity of the video sequence, I will export the video back to my camera roll at the highest-quality settings.

And then I will open up the Gravie text-editing app and add my text overlays.

I prefer to do my text overlays using this app rather than the Splice app (which also supports text overlays) because I find that I have more fine-grained control over the location, the timing, the animation, the font, the color, and any special effects such as fading in and fading out of the text.

When you are happy with your text titles, simply export your finished video to your camera roll. Your Gravie project file is still editable, in case you want to go back and change any of the text.

Variations

Instead of filming video clips, you can instead choose to shoot a recipe sequence as a series of still photos and still be able to assemble the images and text overlays as a video.

You can use the Splice video-editing app to import your shots into a sequence and adjust the timing for each photo. And then export Gravie text app to add the text overlays.

Exercise

Think about a simple dish that you like to make, and then storyboard, set up, shoot, and edit a simple recipe video using your smartphone.

The Bottom Line

Preparation is the key to making a great studio shoot.

CHAPTER 6

Interviews

Effective techniques for preparing and conducting film interviews.

Key Concepts

- Observational narrative
- Interview questions
- Preparing the gear
- Capturing soundbites
- Framing
- Audio
- Log and capture

Online Videos

- Newsmakers in Perugia
- The innovators

Mini Tutorial

- Framing interview subjects

Exercise

- Film an interview

Figure 6.1

ONLINE VIDEOS

Watch the videos for this chapter at www.SmartFilmBook.com.

Goal

Real people talking about real issues can produce compelling scenes and the foundation for strong videos. Interview responses may look easy to produce, but there's a lot that has to go right to get a result on camera.

Challenges

Recording interviews with strangers requires a proper amount of preparation ahead of time, as well as the careful attention and focus at the time of capture to get the best results.

Figure 6.2

ONLINE EXAMPLE 6.1

Newsmakers in Perugia

This illustrated interview style involves a single subject speaking at an event in Perugia, Italy. The soundbite is combined with scenes that show what the subject is describing.

Building Blocks

The foundation for this style of interview segment is the recording of the soundbites of the subject.

After the interview, I filmed scenes at the event that matched up with what the subject spoke about.

Pre-production Planning

There are a few things to prepare before conducting an interview like this.

I wanted the video to be stable, so I attached the phone to a tripod.

Because this was such a noisy environment, I attached a small lapel mic to the subject.

And finally, I had to warm up for the interview by making some small talk and thinking of an open-ended question. An open-ended question allows a subject to speak at length and convey a complete thought.

Location

The International Festival of Journalism in Perugia.

Apps

Filmic Pro, iMovie, Storyo.

Setups

Tripod, Shoulderpod grip to attach phone to tripod, Rode SmartLav+ microphone.

Open-Ended Questions

- Describe for me …
- Could you tell me why?
- What happened here?
- Tell me about …
- What is it like to do this?
- What do you hope to get out of this?

- Why is this important to you?
- What do think will happen to you?
- What do you make of this?
- How will you explain what has happened here to other people?
- What are you worried about?
- What are you telling your children?

Editing the Video

The interview was pretty straightforward because I had prepared my camera, mic, and tripod before approaching the subject.

The only thing I had to do was remember to put my phone into airplane mode and disable notifications. Doing this ensures that interference from the cell phone's radio won't distort the audio being recorded.

I was able to speak with the subject with the camera off for a couple of minutes and explain to him what I was going to do. My on-camera question was "tell me your name and what you are doing here in Perugia."

That is why he opens up introducing himself. I used nonverbal cues while he was talking, to maintain eye contact to let him know that I liked what I was hearing, and to continue. The subject flowed from one thought to the next until he wrapped it up with a nice ending thought.

This clip gave me the foundation for editing the video.

Using the iMovie app I placed that clip onto the primary video track and trimmed it to eliminate the sloppy few seconds before and after recording the take.

With the Storyo app I edited a few of the still pictures together into an animation and saved that as a clip to the camera roll. I then was able to import that into the iMovie project as a cutaway clip that is placed on the video track above the interview soundbite.

I did the same thing with a hyperlapse and a time-lapse clip.

I finished off the project by adding a title card that plays for the first few seconds. I added this clip using the split-screen mode in the iMovie app.

I then added a closing title and a branding logo at the end using the Gravie text app.

Exercise

This style of interviewing where you don't hear the reporter's voice is called an "observational narrative."

It takes some practice to get people comfortable talking to you while they are being filmed.

And they must express their thoughts clearly in complete sentences. Don't worry about editing a video for your exercise. I want you to interview three people and ask each of them a very simple open ended question like: "tell me about what's been going on the last 10 minutes" or "what do you think will happen now that this and this have just taken place?"

These are sample questions you can use to get started making interviews. The only way to make better interviews is to prepare thoroughly ahead of time and then make many short practice interviews.

FRAMING INTERVIEW SUBJECTS

Before filming an interview you need to plan how your subject will look on camera.

This is called "framing," and there are a few things to keep in mind.

To frame great interviews you need to pay attention to:

- Stability
- Shot size
- Background
- Lighting
- Composition
- Subject's eyes

Stability

Interviews are much easier to make when your device is attached to a tripod. This frees up your hands so you can focus on other important tasks.

Shot Size

A medium close-up shot is used to gather responses to interview questions. This size allows the viewer to focus on the subject's face. Remember that the default autofocus and auto exposure modes on mobile devices are unreliable, so be sure to lock your focus and exposure settings before recording.

Background

The background is what the viewer sees behind your subject. Look for a neutral or iconic background to include in your frame. Simpler is always better. Avoid background scenes that are distracting and noisy whenever possible.

Lighting

The viewer needs to clearly see your interview subject's face, so be sure that they are not standing in front of a bright window or in deep shadow. You can use a small reflector or continuous light source to help illuminate your victim's face.

Composition

Turn on the grid in your camera settings app to make it easier to frame the face. Your subject should either be framed up on the right side or on the left side of the screen depending upon which side of the camera you are standing on.

Just remember if a subject is "framed right," you must be standing "camera left." And if they are "framed left," you must be standing "camera right."

Subject's Eyes

Align your subject's eyes on the top horizontal grid line to maintain consistency. It is OK if the top of their head is cropped out if it improves the composition.

No two human heads are the same! It is critical that your subject always looks at you and not the camera. Don't stand too far to the right or left of your camera when filming.

> ### TIP
>
> If you can't see both of your subject's eyes in the frame, then you are standing too far to the side of the camera.

You and your subject need to see eye-to-eye. That means that the camera, your eyes, and your subject's eyes are at about the same level.

If there is a big difference in the height of your subject and yourself, then you will want to film your interview at a table where it will be easier to match up the eyes level with the camera lens.

Camera angles alter the viewer's perception of a character's strength. Film directors know this and use angles to indicate who has the power at any given moment in a movie.

- High angle—Filming from a high angle establishes submissiveness or a lack of power in a scene. Like a child looking up to a parent, this angle communicates weakness.

- Low angle—Filming from a low angle helps to establish a character's dominance in a scene. Like a parent looking down on a child it communicates authority and strength.
- Eye level—When the camera and the subject are at the same level, you are able to film a neutral shot. This is ideal for interviews.

Figure 6.3

ONLINE EXAMPLE 6.2

The Innovators

This four-minute scene features the interview responses from three different subjects who work at a media company in Zagreb, Croatia.

Building Blocks

The interview subjects for this piece are the boss of the company and two employee-innovators who launched a wildly successful new video service call Joom Boos.

The boss was interviewed on a range of subjects over a couple of days, and we actually filmed several hours of interviews with him at various locations in the company and about various topics, but principally around the concept of innovation.

For example:

- "How is the leadership changing?"
- "What do you have to provide for employees?"
- "Which types of program get the best results?"

Location

Zagreb, Croatia.

Lighting

Available light.

Ethics

There's no need to show the interviewer asking the questions because these interviews were conducted in the observational narrative style.

This allows for a seamless flow of the ideas coming from the subjects without an awkward interruption or the use of an artificial story device. I added some text overlays to identify the various people and to set the scene.

Preparation

After getting access and filming interviews with the boss, I asked to be allowed to spend some time with the Joom Boos team and sit with the director and a producer.

When the time was right, I would ask them to spend a few minutes on camera to speak about what they're doing, how they're doing it, and why it is important.

I then filmed a variety of shots of the team working in order to build visual sequences that illustrate the themes from the interview soundbites.

This additional visual reporting and documenting is important to prevent the video from just presenting three talking heads (or—worse—only feature the boss and his talking head!).

Interview segments like this are much more involved than simply asking questions on camera.

Gear

I had several cameras with me on this assignment, an iPhone 6S+ with an anamorphic lens attached as well as an Osmo gimbal cam with a wireless microphone.

Apps

This scene was edited in Final Cut Pro X on a MacBook Air.

Editing the Video

I first auditioned each interview and highlighted the key points by writing them down on an index card with time code so that I could find them later. It may sound really analog and slow, but this method is actually very efficient.

It is critically important to listen closely to the interviewee and make notes as to the first few words of every interesting soundbite.

I did this for each of the three interviews. With my notecards in front of me, I could quickly see a great flow of ideas being expressed from subject to subject.

Only then did I fire up the editing program. The edit was made very quickly because I knew exactly which soundbites I wanted and in what order I wanted them placed.

Once I had built my bed track, I went and found cutaway shots to illustrate the details that were being spoken about.

CHAPTER 7

Livestreaming

Produce live broadcasts.

Key Concepts

- Covering breaking news
- Interviewing officials
- Audience interaction
- Stability
- Sound
- Multi-camera switching
- Live show production

Online Videos

- Breaking news—fire
- Live studio gear test

Gear Tips

- A "go bag" for mobile journalism
- Studio livestreaming with iPhones and iPad

Figure 7.1 Livestream videos can take viewers behind the scenes at an event or "on-set" to a professional quality video production. Reporters commonly produce live broadcasts from scenes of breaking news like this protest in Berlin.

ONLINE VIDEOS

Watch the videos for this chapter at www.SmartFilmBook.com.

Goal

To have a live interactive video experience with your audience using mobile phones.

Challenges

One person produced these examples. Solo production of livestream video is very demanding and just because I have done it as a "proof of concept" doesn't mean that these efforts could not have been improved with the addition of an assistant. Having a partner coordinate some of the tasks would most certainly have improved these reports.

Figure 7.2 A Periscope live video streamed at broadcast quality with an iPhone from a fire scene in Berlin.

ONLINE EXAMPLE 7.1

Breaking News—Fire

Building Blocks

This livestream video transports viewers behind the press line at a breaking news scene—a fire at a department store in downtown Berlin.

It was produced using the Periscope app from Twitter.

Pre-production Planning

As a professional journalist (and having worked as a photojournalist for the Associated Press early in my career) I always keep a packed "go bag" in my studio that will allow me to cover breaking news situations.

My current go bag includes a carbon-fiber tripod, smartphone grip, and a broadcast microphone. I also have a charged-up power bank, and extra cables that I keep in a separate bag inside.

I stow all of this gear in a waterproof backpack so that when the call comes, I can go live in 90 seconds.

Figure 7.3 Robb's "go bag" for broadcasting mobile journalism livestreams: Oakley waterproof backpack, Sevenoak smartphone grip, Sirui tripod, CN-22 face light, Røde reporter mic with i-XLR, IK Multimedia iRig lav mic, power bank, headphones, charging cable (iPhone 6S+ not shown).

Location

Berlin.

Ethics

A live broadcast can be unpredictable in a situation like this because the reporter never knows exactly what will be said and what access they might get.

In addition, the live text notifications from the audience watching the video can be distracting and in some cases annoying, particularly if someone is trolling the livestream.

If someone makes an inappropriate comment you can swipe down on their name to block them from commenting on your broadcast.

Most of the time your interaction with the audience is helpful. If someone proposes a good question that you didn't think to ask, they could be rewarded when you ask it.

Figure 7.4

Preparation

I get an alert from a colleague about smoke coming from a building near the Gendarmenmarkt.

This is about a five-minute bike ride from my flat. Once I arrive at the scene, I lock my bike and quickly attach the phone to the tripod, connect the microphone, check audio levels using Filmic Pro, turn off message notifications, and launch the Periscope app.

I also tweet to my followers that I am about to go live from an event and use the appropriate hash tags.

The Method

It can take a few minutes for an audience to join a livestream, so in this situation I begin with a piece-to-camera set up at the edge of the press line.

I then make my way over to where the fire official is taking reporters' questions.

I know I'm going to pass a scene where firefighters are securing the fire, so I pause there and provide a stable shot of the activity while narrating what I know and don't know yet.

This is where livestreaming with a tripod pays off.

Apps

Periscope, FilmicPro.

Takeaway

You have to love that the fire official (after telling me he doesn't speak English) gives me answers in English and then a running commentary in English.

I am thrilled that the people in my audience that don't speak German can understand what he had just said.

It's also a very funny and revealing moment for the audience to see how a reporter works with officials at a breaking news scene to get the details they would like to know.

Basic Kit for Live Field Reporting

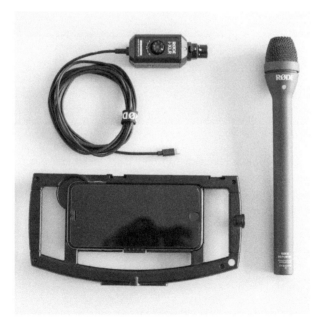

Figure 7.5 Røde reporter mic with i-XLR, and a stable smartphone grip. This low-cost kit will allow you to produce pro-quality live broadcasts while you roam around and interview people at events.

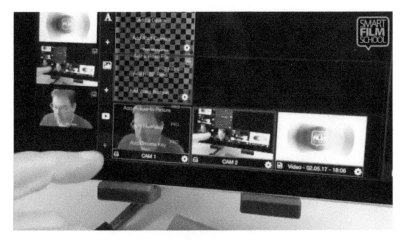

Figure 7.6

ONLINE EXAMPLE 7.2

Live Studio Gear Test

This video is a solo-produced Facebook livestream featuring multi-camera switching, show graphics, and TV-style production.

Building Blocks

At the heart of the system is an iPad Pro running the Live: Air app from Teradek.

Caution. This "free" app features several expensive in-app purchases for unlocking advanced features (for example, I paid $49.99 to remove the Teradek watermark).

The studio cameras are iPhones that have been retired from #MOJO field work.

Camera 1 is an iPhone 6+ that made MOJO reports from over 20 countries over two years.

I attached a small lens from Olloclip to frame the shot for a presenter. Camera 2 is my current #MOJO cam—an iPhone 6S+—placed into an Osmo Mobile rig. I feature the Osmo Mobile in the show.

The iPhone 4S in the teleprompter was brought out of retirement to pair up with the $120 Parrot teleprompter rig. It is running an older version of their app.

This gear—plus a versatile studio design—allows me to quickly produce event videos for webinars, live shows for social streams, and video tutorials for e-learning courses.

Bonus: It's awesome for making Skype calls to your mom.

Let's highlight the essential working parts of building a low-cost live video studio that delivers high-end results without requiring a big crew or typical TV budget.

Setups

Figure 7.7 Here is the gear I use for live studio broadcasts. Note that the computer and screens are only used for monitoring the live broadcast.

All of the live video production is done with a few old iPhones and an iPad Pro.

Teradek's Live: Air app running on the iPad Pro includes all of the basic functionality of a hardware video switcher.

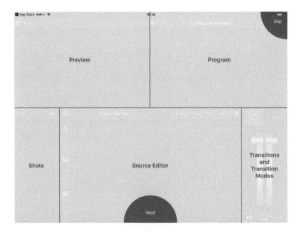

Figure 7.8 A video switcher organizes sources to make shots that you then preview and cut to program. The "program" pane is the only thing the viewer ever sees.

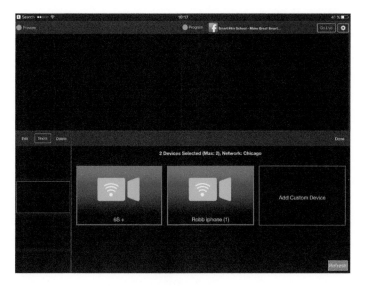

Figure 7.9

1. On the iPad Pro I add iPhone cameras as sources in the Live: Air app.

Figure 7.10

2. I verify that the iPhone is now a live video camera source. The status line shows a healthy connection via the WIFI network. A 3380 kbps data rate allows me to transmit at 1080p HD resolution.

Figure 7.11

3. I build my show by importing more sources: video segments, show graphics, text overlays, and logos. I create a preset for a main shot that combines the feed from camera 1 with the show logo and title text overlay. I continue to make a few more shot preset variations and when the show starts I have only to touch the thumbnail for the shot to load it into preview. NOTE: The show will be more professional-looking if you can have an assistant make the shot transitions rather than trying to do it all yourself while on camera like I did in this "proof of concept" video.

Figure 7.12

4. If your show included the playing of a pre-recorded video clip, be sure to set the video file to "Stop when done" to prevent the clip from looping.

Figure 7.13

5. Set up the livestream for your Facebook page.

Figure 7.14

6. Ta da! Your show will appear live on your Facebook page.

CHAPTER 8

Music Video

Set a film to music.

Key Concepts

- Permissions
- "J" and "L" cuts
- Self-filming
- Process shots
- Improvisation
- Experimental filmmaking

Online Videos

- Am I awake?
- Making of "The ABC Song"

App Tutorial

- Introduction to LumaFusion video editor

Figure 8.1

ONLINE VIDEOS

Watch the videos for this chapter at www.SmartFilmBook.com.

Music videos are a popular form of film expression. Often these are character-driven mini films or a recreation of a musical performance. We look at these two primary forms in this chapter.

Goal

Making an original film for a piece of music is a great way to explore the art of filmmaking. There really are no rules and you can follow your muse and pursue experimental cinematic ideas that you would not otherwise be allowed to use for corporate or editorial projects.

Challenges

Getting permission to use a piece of music for commercial filmmaking can be a real challenge. It is never OK to use copyrighted music without permission or without paying license fees to the rights holders.

Figure 8.2

ONLINE EXAMPLE 8.1

Am I Awake?

This music video is a walking dream sequence filmed in Cologne, Germany. The music is by Brooklyn-based band They Might Be Giants, who invited filmmakers to make a music video for their song "Am I Awake?".

Building Blocks

I was working in Cologne at RTL TV studios teaching video production to a group of international journalists for 10 days. In my time off I found myself filming at strange hours of the day as I ventured out to discover the pulse of the city.

I had been cutting these disconnected shots together each night in my hotel room to make a scene sketchbook. I was planning to only share those moments with my students until I noticed on Facebook that two of my favorite songsmiths, "the two Johns" from "They Might Be Giants," had announced a filmmaker's contest for their tune "Am I Awake?".

Figure 8.3 From time to time, the band They Might Be Giants invite filmmakers to freely use their music as a soundtrack to make original films and enter them in a contest. The winning film becomes the official music video for the track and the director is paid.

I had never heard this track before, and I said to myself, "what the heck?" I was inspired because they were granting filmmakers a license to use their music to make an original film and you had complete creative control.

I dropped their music track onto my Final Cut Pro X timeline to see if their music matched these strange sequences I was recording, and it pretty much was a lock. The musicians use personal imagery in their lyrics and clever rhythms in their beats that aligned quite nicely with the eclectic shots I had filmed.

Location

Cologne, Germany.

Lighting

Available light.

Props and Gear

Found objects. Tram rides. I attached my camera to a Pico dolly to film low-angle motion shots. This low-cost table dolly looks like a skateboard. I attached a string to it to make it move.

Ethics

The artists had invited filmmakers to make a movie using their music, so I was free to explore the marriage of my pictures and their words, and share it as part of the competition. They offered their music for free download to filmmakers on Soundcloud. I didn't win the contest, but that doesn't mean I am not happy with the resulting film.

Preparation

After seeing the results from my test shots working with the soundtrack, I spent more time in Cologne filming night scenes, the salsa dancing scene, and the morning coffee ritual at my friend's house. Those additional scenes helped answer the question posed in the song's title: "Am I Awake?"

Apps

iMovie, Final Cut Pro.

Storyboard

I opened with a night shot filmed on a tram to match the rapid beats that start the song and then transitioned to a pre-dawn sequence of me walking on Cologne's iconic bridge. I keep alternating between selfies, tram shots, and POV (point-of-view) shots to establish a theme of me essentially sleepwalking as I move between locations.

The elasticity of night and day is explored by filming at odd hours of the day and this pattern continues through tours along the tram line and to a nightclub full of salsa dancers until it finally ends up inside a flat where coffee is being made.

Takeaway

I grew up as a teenager when MTV music television launched, so it was a particular thrill to get to make a film for musicians I first discovered way back then. I love the music from these songwriters and they always have made incredible, visually adventurous videos.

OK, so maybe I do wish that I had won the contest after all.

Nah, the money the band offered as a prize would not have been as rewarding as seeing my film airing on MTV.

Figure 8.4

ONLINE EXAMPLE 8.2

Making of "The ABC Song"

The making of a music video can sometimes be as entertaining as the official video.

Building Blocks

I encountered this scene one Saturday morning after leading a film walk for journalists at a media forum in Lviv, Ukraine. I could see from the activity on the square that some professional filmmaking might be happening.

Location

Lviv, Ukraine.

Lighting

Available light.

Props

The singers were wearing traditional costumes but were performing a modern song. The little white beat box at their feet is a critical detail.

Ethics

I approached the crew and asked the director if I could stay close and film their production. I reassured him I would be out of his way and all of his shots.

They were happy to have me film what are essentially "process shots." Process shots reveal the craft of filmmaking—in them the viewer sees the director, the camera, and other production artifacts.

Process shots are commonly used in documentary filmmaking to strengthen the credibility of the reporting by being transparent.

Preparation

I had to make sure that I had a good battery charge to film enough useful footage. Also my camera app was acting up when I attached my microphone and I was worried that the singing would not be captured clearly.

I didn't have time to get my backup mic from the hotel room, or do extensive debugging in the field, so I made sure to make several small recordings of each of the main choir's performances.

I was lucky that they asked the singers to make many takes. This allowed me to move round and film the same musical phrase from many different camera positions.

Apps

Filmic Pro, LumaFusion.

Setups

iPhone 6S+, mini tripod and Sevenoak smartphone grip, Røde VideoMicro microphone.

Storyboard

This is a short film and a very simple scene. I only am showing what the "ABC" means for the song title (using text overlays), and how the singers had to repeat the phrase many times for the film crew.

To add interest, I show shots of the crowd reacting, other things happening at the public square, and the filmmakers operating a drone camera.

Editing the Video

To transfer my shots to my preferred editing device, I "air dropped" the video clips from my iPhone to an iPad Pro where I could edit the video with the LumaFusion app. Air drop is a wireless transfer feature for iOS devices.

Figure 8.5 I detached the audio from the video clip (the green bar) so that I could extend the audio underneath the next clip. This is a called an "L" cut because of the visual shape of how the tracks look on the timeline.

The purpose of this edit is to create a smooth transition for a viewer between shots.

Figure 8.6 The other way to smooth an audio track is to use a "J" cut. This is seen above with the audio (green bar) being heard audible before the next clip is shown.

I also did a little special effect on the last shot. I split the final clip at the final seven seconds and applied a soft focus effect to just that portion of the clip.

Figure 8.7 This small Gaussian blur effect helps to create the feeling of completion. Simply double click on an any clip in LumaFusion to enter the clip editor and tap on the color and effects icons to open a pane where special effects menus are located.

The icon of the water drop is the blur effect pane where you can audition different styles of blurring.

Figure 8.8 I also retimed this clip to half speed by tapping on the speed and reverse icon and moving the slider to the left.

This soft and slow ending was where I placed my branding text overlay. The contrast between the sharp edges of the type and the soft-focus video make the text easy to read.

If I had not done this, then it may not have been so clear to the viewer because of the complexity of the image.

CHAPTER 9

360° VR Video

Film and edit spherical video.

Key Concepts

- Best practices for 360° filming
- How 360° video works
- Story planning
- Production values

Online Videos

- 360° surf school
- 5 tips for filming in 360°

Guide

- 5 tips for filming in 360°

App Tutorial

- LumaFusion

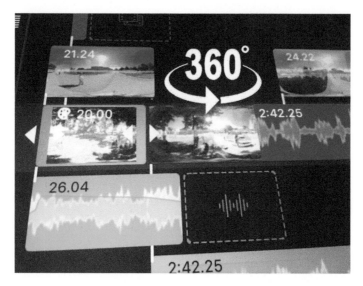

Figure 9.1 360° VR video is a popular type of filmmaking that can be produced for low-budget and high-budget productions.

There are several high-resolution, self-stitching 360° cameras on the market for less than US$400 dollars and new models are arriving on the scene that support live broadcasts and immersive 360° audio.

ONLINE VIDEOS

Watch the videos for this chapter at www.SmartFilmBook.com.

What Makes 360° VR Video Attractive?

Spherical videos simply provide a unique perspective.

Location

360° video provides a sense of space with the viewer being able to look around to get a fuller picture.

Presence

The reporter or presenter's presence can help the viewer understand the story better and provide a focal point.

Immersion

360° scenes that also feature binaural and immersive ambisonic surround audio mixes can bring a heightened sense of emotion, empathy, and involvement.

Keys to the Style

- Directing attention with on-screen graphics and the use of a presenter.
- Avoiding close-up shots and cutaways.
- Avoiding camera movement.
- Multi-channel audio mixing and sound design.

Figure 9.2 You can see a great example of these elements in the first example video.

ONLINE EXAMPLE 9.1

360° Surf School (With Kyle Thiermann, Discovery VR)

Link to view on YouTube: www.youtube.com/watch?v=lgyVVoyGRIo.

Building Blocks

This is a straightforward instructional video with a clear beginning, middle, and end.

- Thiermann provides a technical briefing from the shore. The camera is on a tripod, he can be clearly understood, and on-screen graphics clue the viewer in to specific things he wants to highlight.
- He then paddles out to the breaking waves. The camera is mounted to the surfboard and the viewer is shown the proper technique.

- Thiermann starts to surf in to shore and explains how surfers are supposed to give way to others when riding the waves. The camera is handheld.
- On a cliff above the shore, he summarizes the experience. Camera is back on the tripod.

Location

Santa Cruz, California.

Lighting

Available.

Ethics

The underwater bubbling sounds at 01:32 seem out of place, because all of the action on screen is happening above the waterline. This canned sound effect does not match the video.

The fix is to record the sound of him paddling in the water separately from the same location and then mix that sound in later with the voice-over narration. That would more faithfully recreate the soundscape.

Thiermann makes a mistake by blocking another surfer's right of way and points out the error. This is a great moment in the film and helps to show how tricky surfing can be.

Preparation

The filmmakers had a plan. They had a script, or at least some talking points sketched out in order to make a clean production. Good microphone technique is used to capture clear audio.

Choosing a camera rig with waterproof camera modules allowed filming of water scenes without damage.

Editing the Video

This multi-camera rig produces several video clips that have to be stitched together and corrected using software running on a desktop computer.

The on-screen graphics also are three-dimensional, which further indicates that a modern 360° video editing app was used.

The Bottom Line

Even though the video is fairly short, the effective use of a strong central character, solid story planning, and commitment to production values combine to make a highly effective and entertaining experience.

How 360° Video Works

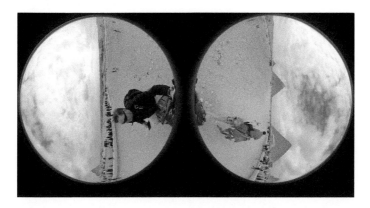

Figure 9.3 Spherical video as seen by the two lenses of a Theta S 360° camera.

The two images inside these circles have to be "stitched" together in software to produce an equi-rectangular image. A camera like the Theta S does this with software running inside the camera.

Figure 9.4

The resulting still frames or video footage can then be edited with a video editor that supports a 2:1 aspect ratio.

ONLINE EXAMPLE 9.2

5 Tips for Filming in 360°

1 Keep the Sun on the Side

When framing your shot, take care to ensure that the sun is somewhere between the lenses and that neither one is pointed directly at it. When a lens faces the sun, it receives much more light than the other side and this often results in a visible halo that reveals the stitching line.

Figure 9.5

2 Use a Selfie Stick or Small Tripod

If you want to avoid taking photos that all have a giant thumb in them, you will need to attach a selfie stick or a small tripod to the 360° camera.

The slimmer the mount the better.

3 Avoid the Extreme Close-Up

For the same reason that the big thumb can be distracting, you will want to keep subjects' faces a certain distance away from the camera lenses too.

Make some test shots with your rig to find the right distance. Look for faces that are not distorted from the visual stitching that happens in the software.

4 Use a Remote Control App

You can film professional-looking VR images once you get your 360° camera in an interesting location, have it stabilized on a stick or tripod, and can activate it remotely.

Most cameras ship with a companion smartphone app that allows you to trip the shutter or toggle the video camera on and off.

5 Watch the Horizon

It is critical to get the horizon level when filming landscape shots.

Figure 9.6 Pay attention to the "verticality" of your camera rig and double check the horizon with the live image preview with your smartphone app.

FILMING IN 360°

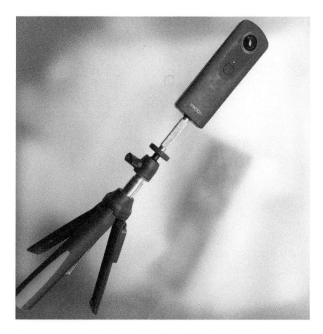

Figure 9.7 The Theta S rig I use to film mobile 360° photos and videos. It helps to use a slender tripod and an extension rod to keep the tripod as small as possible in the final images.

Transferring Files From the Theta S

With the Theta S, the images and clips are stored on the camera and can be wirelessly transferred to your smartphone using the Theta S mobile app.

It can take several minutes to transfer video clips, so plan ahead and don't record long scenes if you intend to edit the video on your smartphone with an app like LumaFusion.

For example, you can make a one-minute test recording to begin with.

Figure 9.8

Editing 360° Video With the V360° App

V360° was the first 360° video editing app for smartphones. It runs on both iOS and Android, and provides a very simple editing workflow for adding and trimming clips.

The Android version of the app has additional features and the developers promise to bring them to the iOS version.

The advanced editing features include:

- Specifying the heading of the video (what the viewer first sees)
- Titles
- Transitions
- Adding credits for your video

The ability to tune the heading of the video is a really nice touch.

A preview of the app features: https://www.youtube.com/watch?v=2oDY8tw2du8.

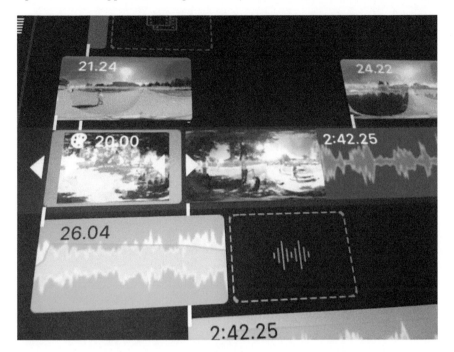

Figure 9.9

Editing Theta S 360° Video in LumaFusion App

The LumaFusion video editor app offers more fine-grained control over the audio tracks, graphics overlays, transitions, and titling.

The current version does not allow you to change the initial heading a viewer will see, so using a directional text or graphic overlay is a good idea.

Here is a quick-start guide to using the app.

1. Open the app and create a new project by tapping on the + icon.

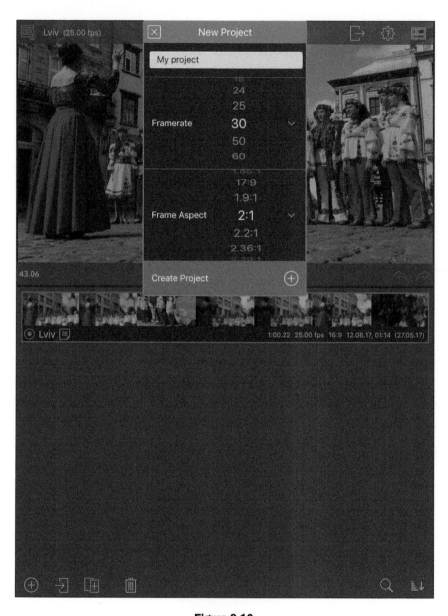

Figure 9.10

2. Select the 2:1 frame aspect from the slider.

Figure 9.11

3. Select a 360° video clip from the camera roll and drop it to the timeline. You can now trim it and edit it just like a regular video clip.

Figure 9.12

4. Add music or record voice-over narration and adjust the timing and volume levels on the timeline. The app includes royalty-free music that you can use to improve your masterpiece.

Figure 9.13

5. You can create a 360° video using the equi-rectangular photos that the camera captures instead of the video clips. Notice how much higher the quality is for the still frames. I added the 360° logo to the timeline by placing the image on the track above the first video clip. This provides a directional clue to the viewer.

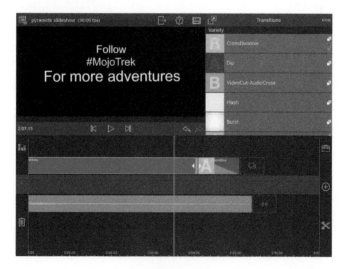

Figure 9.14

6. As a finishing step you can add text overlays and position them in the video.

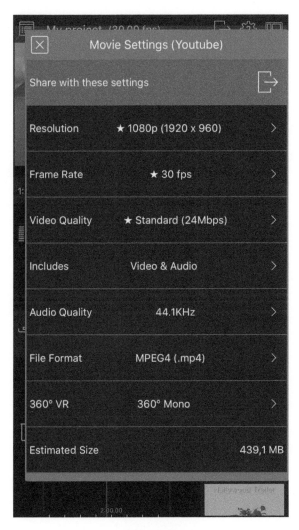

Figure 9.15

7. Export your 360° video at the highest resolution and select "360° Mono" as the VR output setting. Your video will be rendered and saved to your camera roll with the metadata injected. This means that the video will play properly on social media platforms like YouTube and Facebook.

Check out the in-depth video tutorials featuring the LumaFusion video-editing app at www.smartfilmschool.com to take a deeper dive into editing 360° video projects.

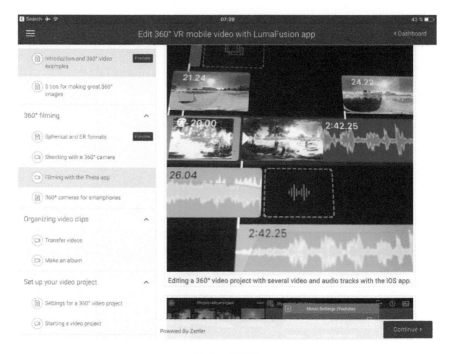

Figure 9.16

CHAPTER 10

Nature

Filming dynamic natural landscapes in the great outdoors.

Key Concepts

- Location research
- Natural sound
- Special equipment
- Glance—object
- Avoiding other tourists

Online Videos

- Flamingo sunrise
- Across the Alps
- Ocean waves

Mini Tutorials

- Aspect ratios
- Filming with an anamorphic lens

App Tips

- Final Cut Pro X

Exercise

- Film a nature scene

Figure 10.1 A great outdoors film is not only inspired by nature, but faithfully transmits the sights and sounds to make a viewer feel as if they are part of the scene.

ONLINE VIDEOS

Watch the videos for this chapter at www.SmartFilmBook.com.

Goal

By the end of this chapter you should know what fundamentals to focus on when filming a nature scene.

Challenges

One of the biggest challenges to filming a good nature scene is getting access to wild animals and other natural wonders.

Another challenge can be setting your alarm clock early enough so that you are in a good filming position very early in the morning. That certainly was the first challenge to overcome in the making of this first lesson video.

Figure 10.2

ONLINE EXAMPLE 10.1

Flamingo Sunrise

The important thing to notice about this film is how continuity is established and maintained between the alternating shots of the birds and the observer.

Building Blocks

This film features an extended sequence of time spent with flamingos in a saltwater lake in Chile as well as a woman who is observing them with field glasses.

There are scenes of peak action with birds flying as well as passive shots with the observer watching the birds grazing for saltwater shrimp.

The flying shots are used as entrances and exits into the setting where the flamingos feed each morning at dawn.

Pre-production Planning

This location is a remote nature reserve about an hour's drive from San Pedro de Atacama. There was no opportunity for scouting this film location before the shoot.

But that is not to say we had arrived unprepared.

This location was one of the highlights of our pre-trip research. In our reading, we had noted that we would be visiting at a time of the year when the flamingos would also be there.

Our interviews with local experts further revealed that the best time to arrive would be before dawn. The flamingos feed at first light and that would provide the best possible opportunity to get close to them to film with a wide-angle lens.

Location

Reserva Nacionel Los Flamencos, Salar de Atacama. This vast natural reserve in Chile's Atacama Desert is the temporary home of migratory flamingos. It is in this giant salt lake that they feed off the brine shrimp that turns their feathers pink.

Lighting

Available light. No reflectors or artificial light sources used.

We were lucky to find that the dawn light was softly diffused by a marine layer and reflected beautifully on the salt-water surface.

A Prop as a Narrative Device

The red lens field glasses lend an iconic and stylish visual element to the piece. They become the visual identity for the observer and make for a memorable close-up.

Figure 10.3 These "red lenses" are featured in the opening and closing shots.

You may also notice that in the last shot, the photographer suddenly becomes the "observer."

This juxtaposition was discovered in the edit and adds some character intrigue. Furthermore a sense of mystery and suspense is created by simply never revealing the face of the observer.

This was an intentional decision to frame the faces always being blocked by the red lenses. This creates suspense and also suggests that the filmmaker perhaps is also just another observer.

Filming shot variations with the same red lenses allowed for new story connections to be discovered later in the edit.

Making even small connections between humans and the awesomeness of nature makes the scene more compelling to watch—more compelling because the viewers can imagine themselves standing at that alien shore watching wild flamingos fly above them. Ultimately, they feel as if they have become the observer.

Preparation

The observer/photo model in this scene is also my wife and travel companion for our 30-day four-wheel-drive film trek across the Atacama Desert.

Our "flamingo film plan" required us to be at the gates of the nature reserve at least 30 minutes before the rangers arrived.

We wanted to be there at the best time to observe the flamingos and also to have the chance to be set up and filming the birds before the rumbling vans carrying loud-talking tourists (which we suspected would soon arrive) trampled over the inherent tranquility of the scene.

The night before the shoot I assembled and tested the film rig. I made sure that the phone battery and the power bank were charged up, and that the anamorphic settings were all made for Filmic Pro app.

I also ensured that we had fuel in the four-wheel-drive as well as fresh food and coffee supplies for spending the day away from our campsite.

Figure 10.4 Making coffee at the park entrance.

Figure 10.5 Arriving at the gate before the rangers opened the park allowed me to be the first to gain access and have some quiet time filming the flamingos.

Figure 10.6

Figure 10.7 10 minutes later, the park was full of chatty tourists. I filmed them too.

Figure 10.8 And then Jördis and I cooked breakfast at the ranger station.

Figure 10.9

Apps

Filmic Pro and Splice video editor.

Setups and Rigs

In the gear settings of the Filmic Pro app I created a new preset to use with the Moondog Labs anamorphic lens. I set the app for 1080p resolution and 50 frames per second. I used the higher frame rate in order to capture smoother video. Filming at higher frame rates also allows you to slow down any section of the video and still maintain high quality.

Note that the camera is a little bit out of focus in a couple of the shots in my sequence.

This is because the BeastGrip Pro mount that I used to mate the Moondog lens to my iPhone is a little bit fragile.

Or maybe it is only fragile when taking it into the bumpy backcountry tracks of northern Chile. It happens that with a lot of four-wheel-drive travel, the tiny hex head screws easily come loose and upset the focus.

ONLINE EXAMPLE 10.2

Across the Alps

Having a rigid, simple, and shockproof rig for your phone turns out to be a big deal.

I now film backcountry scenes with a Helium Core iPhone rig cage. This cage is machined to fit each specific iPhone model, and as a result has fewer moving parts (see https://heliumcine.com).

There is little chance for the anamorphic lens to move out of focus with this setup.

Figure 10.10 This sturdy camera cage solution served us well for a week-long film trek in the Austrian Alps.

Figure 10.11 The small cage allowed for reliable filming at altitude.

Figure 10.12 It is rugged enough to survive being stuffed into a backpack during days of high mountain scrambling and non-stop rain trekking between Alpine huts.

Figure 10.13 I also used my rig for filming an interview with the man who lives with his family at the Freiburger Hütte. His family serves summer hikers with food and lodging every day as they make their tours between the peaks. A Røde video mic and a lightweight tripod attach easily to the Helium cage to support high-quality recording of the interview.

Figure 10.14 The rig can also be used handheld out on the trail and still yield good results.

Figure 10.15 The 4K video clips can be edited each evening inside the hut using the LumaFusion video editing app by LumaTouch.

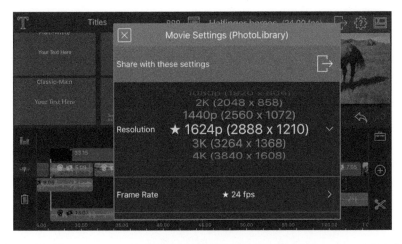

Figure 10.16 And then exported to the camera roll at a slightly lower resolution for uploading to YouTube and Facebook.

I never had to leave the mountains to shoot, edit, and share cinematic scenes in 4K quality with my audience.

My Beastgrip Pro rig is now retired from field duty and serves as a dedicated rig in my Berlin studio. I use it to attach my vintage Nikon lenses to an iPhone to make some truly unique studio portraits.

Aspect Ratios

Filmmakers use different aspect ratios when filming to reach different audiences.

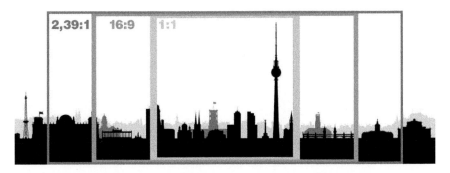

Figure 10.17 These are some commonly used formats today for digital filmmaking: 16:9 (digital television); 1:1 (social video); 2.39:1 (cinema projection).

You may have noticed that the films in the chapter were made in the 2.39:1 widescreen format using anamorphic lenses for filming.

The videos were not cropped to this shape. The shape is a result of using anamorphic distortion lenses for filming and software that undistorted the scene on playback.

Figure 10.18 Moondog Labs make an anamorphic lens that you can attach to your smartphone to simulate the widescreen look made popular by Panavision.

The 40mm Panavision anamorphic lens beloved by film directors has a 40mm vertical field of view but a 20mm horizontal field of view.

This distortion lens squeezes more visual information from the sides and sends this to the camera sensor.

Figure 10.19 An anamorphic lens optically squeezes a wider field of view to fit to the camera sensor.

Figure 10.20 This distortion can be digitally de-squeezed by a camera app like Filmic Pro.

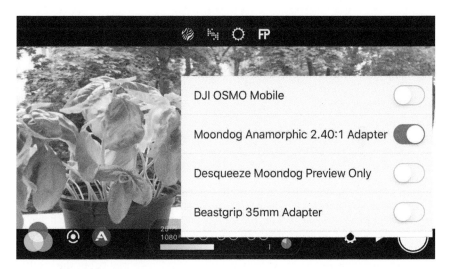

Figure 10.21 In Filmic Pro, you can select a hardware setting for the Moondog Lab lens that will digitally "de-squeeze" your video to produce a non-distorted widescreen version.

Figure 10.22 Films shot with anamorphic lenses have an organic "look" that other lenses don't capture.

These lenses are popular with top filmmakers like Wes Anderson because they capture a subconscious "3D quality" that invokes a heightened sense of reality.

Figure 10.23 Anamorphic lenses produce artifacts like aberrations, long horizontal lens flares, oval bokeh, vignetting, and spherical curving. Those may sound like reasons to avoid this kind of lens, but they all add up to making a very watchable widescreen experience.

You can crop a high-resolution video file to the 2.39:1 aspect ratio, but the results will not look the same.

Editing a Rough Cut of the Scene

This scene in Lesson Film 10.1 of the flamingos is actually just a sketch or a "first assembly," it's not the finished version, but all the shots are locked in place on the timeline to tell a visual story.

Figure 10.24

What you may notice in a first assembly is that the shot sequences are established but more polishing steps still need to happen. For example, the soundtrack is uneven in levels and quality.

The audio levels from the natural sounds will need to be extended and cross-faded across the shots to provide a more continuous soundscape experience for the viewer.

Takeaway

With a little ingenuity and perseverance, you can capture scenes of cinema quality without having to secure special access or have a crew lug around heavy camera gear.

With apps like LumaFusion video editor, you can also edit your movie at the campsite and never actually have to leave the great outdoors.

Exercise

Make a plan. Get up early. Go to a national park you have always wanted to visit. Prepare to stay awhile. Observe the best times to film and then make your kit ready.

Be prepared to outwit fellow tourists, and possibly annoy your partner to angle in and outmaneuver the elements in order to get the shots that others wished they had made.

Overall, be patient. Nature unfolds on her own timetable. If things don't work out on your first attempt, at least you can enjoy the outdoors while you plan and make your next film adventures.

LESSON FILM 10.3

Ocean Waves

This 11-hour movie was assembled from audio recordings and video clips recorded with an iPhone at two remote beaches: one in Florida and one in Chile.

Figure 10.25

Building Blocks

The first elements of this movie's production began with sound recordings that were made at a remote beach on the Atlantic Ocean with an iPhone and a shotgun microphone.

Additional sound recordings were made with an iPhone and an omnidirectional microphone at an isolated beach on the Pacific Ocean.

The images are a mix of panoramic still frame shots as well as anamorphic shots filmed with the Moondog Labs lens adapter.

All of these iPhone assets were transferred to a Mac and edited in Final Cut Pro because that desktop video-editing application can be used to build a movie of 11 hours running time.

Location

Pan de Azúcar Beach, Chile, and Playalinda Beach, Canaveral Nation Seashore, Florida.

These remote natural locations can take quite a while to reach and also require special permission from the park rangers.

We had to purchase a backcountry permit at each location to be allowed access to these isolated areas.

Fun Fact

Pan de Azúcar Beach on the Pacific Ocean (26.1776° S, 70.5495° W) is located east of Playalinda Beach on the Atlantic Ocean (28.6555° N, 80.6318° W). This perspective can be quite disorienting for an American like me!

Figure 10.26

Ethics

This is an 11-hour movie reconstruction; it is not an 11-hour recording.

These are the authentic sounds and sights recorded from two locations and the film composite faithfully represents what you would see and hear if you were left alone at an ocean beach for an entire summer day without encountering any other tourists.

Note that there are a few audio giggles from me and my wife that were recorded, and I decided to include those moments because this is a personal film made just for us.

It is both our "Apple TV screensaver video" and the soundtrack we play every evening while sleeping.

Figure 10.27 Exporting the 11-hour video from Final Pro X took several hours.

Preparation

After having visited Playalinda Beach a few years ago, I decided that if I had the chance to return I would bring a good microphone and reserve enough time to be able to make long-playing sound recordings.

Gear

iPhone 6 in airplane mode, Røde NTG 4+ shotgun microphone with "dead cat" windscreen, IK multimedia iRig Pro XLR interface.

Recently I have been using the Shure Motiv MV88 digital microphone for nature recordings and it has a great app with really pro sound-recording settings.

When it comes to making good sound recordings in nature, and in particular at windy locations like shorelines, the decision to use a high-quality microphone and quiet preamp interface becomes critical.

Putting the phone into airplane mode disables the cellular radio, which can cause interference and unwanted audio artifacts while recording.

Apps

I like to use the AudioCopy app because it's free and it's very simple and it works beautifully with the gear I described above.

I just make sure that whatever app I'm using to record is set at the highest quality—the best resolution and saving the files in a lossless format like WAV.

Some apps offer light compression or limiting to make sure that the signal does not overload the inputs and cause clipping distortion.

Recording the Audio

At each beach, I recorded sound from several locations in the same way a filmmaker shoots different shot sizes when filming a sequence. I recorded 20-minute sections of "close-up" audio right over the waves as well as "wide angle" audio 10 meters from the shore.

I also recorded a 20-minute audio segment near a location where seagulls were gathering.

Recording the Video

I filmed video at 4K resolution at 24 frames per second using the Filmic Pro app on my iPhone. The phone was mounted in a Beastgrip pro with the Moondog Labs anamorphic lens adapter. I also filmed a number of panorama shots using the built-in camera app.

Figure 10.28

Editing the Video

The lesson video was edited in Final Cut Pro X on a Mac. All of the audio files were transferred to the Mac via Airdrop and the high-resolution video files via USB cable with the Image Capture app.

The audio clips were the first elements to be added to the timeline.

They are shown below the video clips. These were trimmed and crossfaded to provide a slowly evolving soundscape that recreates the changing sounds you hear at a wild beach.

The volume levels were adjusted to help make the transitions sound more natural.

Variations

Of course, a shorter film project can be edited in much the same way using the LumaFusion app on an iPad. LumaFusion is a full-featured app that supports multiple video tracks and audio tracks.

CHAPTER 11

Promotional

Make a persuasive pitch with words and pictures.

Key Concepts

- Script writing
- Teleprompter
- Three-point lighting
- Piece-to-camera
- Cutaway shots
- Live photos
- Advanced filmmaking

Online Videos

- Personal appeal—online instructor pitch
- Promoting a business—pottery-making lessons

Mini Tutorial

- Aspect ratios
- Filming with an anamorphic lens

Exercise

- Film a scripted "piece-to-camera" clip

Figure 11.1 A promotional video is a highly visual sales pitch that can be used to market products, services, and shops.

ONLINE VIDEOS

Watch the videos for this chapter at www.SmartFilmBook.com.

Goal

Marketing yourself or your business in video can be a very attractive way to reach new customers.

Challenges

There are many technical challenges to creating a scripted promotional video and sometimes the best way to sell a product is to not approach the project like it is a sales pitch at all. In this chapter I will show two approaches.

Figure 11.2

ONLINE EXAMPLE 11.1

Personal Appeal — Online Instructor Pitch

The purpose of this promotional video is to encourage viewers to enroll in an online course.

Building Blocks

The foundation for this video is a scripted narration delivered directly to the camera.

A "piece-to-camera" is the English phrase that describes the primary footage recorded for this instructor promo video.

It certainly looks like a "selfie" because the person is looking straight at the camera and a good on-camera performance is vital for conveying trust.

An effective instructor promotion involves many layers of supporting information such as the actual course design and sales page. This video promo is designed to work in concert with these other materials and must make a good first impression about the topic and the person teaching it.

A Classic Approach

Reading a script from a teleprompter camera rig is a common video technique commonly used in television and film production. This technique is a great method for capturing an authentic performance.

I used an old iPhone and a Parrot teleprompter connected to a DSLR for my setup.

Location

Studio.

Lighting

Classic three-point lighting with a key, fill, and hair light is used to capture a lifelike portrait.

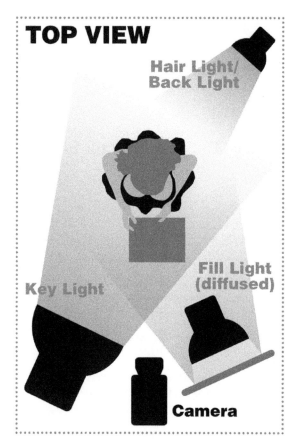

Figure 11.3

Props

A black background and a solid, neutral shirt color help to frame the viewer's attention on the performer's face, and in particular the eyes.

Preparation

This video begins with a script that employs an AIDA sequence:

A—attention
I—interest
D—desire
A—action

This is a popular approach to organize an effective marketing pitch and a good starting point for organizing script ideas.

A lot of visual research and additional filming accompanied the script writing to support and inform these four AIDA goals.

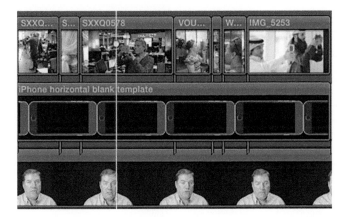

Figure 11.4

For a promo script the main sections are:

Introduction: ATTENTION

A simple introduction by the instructor about themselves and the topic to establish credibility and signal to the viewer that this is the right person to teach this topic.

Benefits: INTEREST

Describe the benefits of your approach and what viewers will be able to do or accomplish after participating or buying from you.

Topics: DESIRE

Explain how the procedure, product, or service is designed and structured. Describe your target viewer. Who should be taking the course and sharing this offer with others?

Enroll: ACTION

Call the viewer to act, share, enroll, subscribe, or buy what you are selling. Invite them to a free webinar, or a free preview of your lesson content.

This is a sample storyboard template for a 90-second promotional video.

	SCENE / SHOTS	NARRATION	DURATION
	Topic:		
	Instructor:		
1	Start with a slide showing your course image placeholder or branding.	Music to match an animation is OK. (This allows the student to maximize the video player and adjust volume level)	3 seconds
2	**Welcome** Give a one sentence intro to the course then tell the student why you're a credible instructor. SHOTS Talking head standup (a "piece to camera" showing instructor). Include cutaway shots to show details and processes.	"Welcome to the XXX Course. Where you will learn to XXX and XXX for XXX. My name is XXX and I'll be leading you through the course. I began my career as a XXX, but soon transitioned to an XX where I XXX. Currently I XXXX for XXXX where I work on XXX."	20 sec
3	**Benefits** Describe the benefits of the course and what students will be able to do after completing it. SHOTS Talking head standup (a "piece to camera" showing instructor). Include cutaway shots to show details and processes you teach. Show shots of you teaching, if you have them!	"I designed this course for anyone who wants to XXX. At the end of this course you will be able to XXX, XXX and XXX for XXX." or "At the end of this course, you'll be able to produce XXXX for XXX.	20 sec
4	**List Major Components** Explain how the course is designed and list (don't describe) the major topics you'll cover. SHOTS Talking head standup with cutaway shots of teaching or screen grabs animations from lectures.	"Ill be teaching a method for XXX called XXX. This method will yield good results in XXX days or less. This method is great for XXX or XXX or even XXX XXX XX XXXX. "We'll go over XXX, the XXX, XXX, XXX, XXX, the XXX you need for XXX and XXX." I will walk you through the entire process, step-by-step."	20 sec
5	**Ideal Student** Describe your target student SHOTS Talking head standup with cutaway shots (Ideally of students in your class.)	"I designed this course for the XXX who wants XX to get XXX about XXX, but struggles with XXXX that are XXX and XXX." Or "The ideal student for this course is an XXX or a XX who wants to expand their skills or launch a XX of their own. " There are no requirements to enroll. "	15 sec
6	**Thank You and Call to Action** Call the student to enroll in the course or try the free preview if they want to explore further. SHOTS Talking head standup with cutaway shots.	"Feel free to look through the course description and we'll see you inside."	10 sec
7	End with your title animation	Music to match an animation is OK.	3 sec

Figure 11.5

App

Parrot teleprompter.

Figure 11.6

Setups

A teleprompter projects the script on a special pane of glass positioned in front of the camera.

The camera lens is at the same level as the performer's eyes. A high-quality microphone is used to capture the audio with the highest fidelity. For my rig, I use a Røde Filmmaker wireless mic kit.

The Script

> Welcome to the Smart Film School where you will learn how to make incredible videos with your smartphone.

My name is Robb Montgomery and I'll be leading you through this course. For the last 10 years I have trained thousands of people like you how to shoot, edit, and share amazing video stories.

These video training courses are used by reporters at CNN, The New York Times, Reuters, and the BBC.

I teach video storytelling at FH Journalism School (Vienna) and the Danish School of Journalism (Copenhagen).

From 1990 to 2005, I worked as a visual editor in the newsrooms of the Chicago Tribune and Chicago Sun-Times.

Smart Film School courses are designed to help you get professional results every time.

This Mobile Journalism course is mandatory for every student studying journalism at the EFJ School in France.

In this quick course you will gain the confidence to become a better video storyteller in less than 30 minutes.

You will learn how to set up your smartphone as a video camera, how to frame and film shots properly, and how to use a simple video-editing app to make amazing video stories that you can share in chat apps, on Facebook, and on YouTube.

If you want to learn how to make professional videos for your company, or develop a freelance career as a videographer, or just become the best filmmaker in your family, then this course is the perfect place to start.

Smart Film School courses take the confusion out of video production by focusing on the fundamentals and guiding you through each step. The lessons are structured to allow you to practice each new skill until it becomes second nature.

So what are you waiting for?

Register now for this introductory course and begin your journey as a video storyteller.

Script Formatting

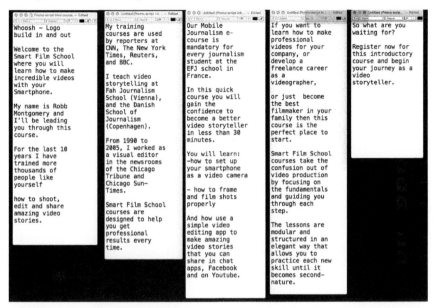

Figure 11.7 Using a word processor, I like to format the script into a narrow column to simulate how it might appear on a teleprompter. I insert an extra line of space between thoughts to indicate a breath space.

Three words per line is the industry standard for a script read. That is the normal pace of speech and it provides you with a handy estimate for how long the video will be because each line represents one second of recording time.

All you have to do is narrow the margins on your word processor document to achieve this preview.

Filming the Video

It can take some time to set up the studio, camera, lighting, microphone, backdrop, and teleprompter.

I often make a few test recordings until I find the right settings.

This discipline also gives me the advantage of rehearsing the script a few times and polishing any words that I may be struggling with as I read from the teleprompter.

I stop filming once I've recorded a good performance all the way through. Sometimes this can be a first take and sometimes it can be a fourth take, it all depends. It can be especially helpful to have a trusted partner behind the lens to keep you in the proper frame of mind as you are performing your script for the camera.

One Perfect Take

I want one clean take to take into the edit. I don't want to waste time trying to piece together the best phrases from multiple takes. That approach may sound simple, but in reality that type of workflow creates an editing headache.

If you are having trouble reading a 90-second script in one take, then take a look at the script. You may be using fancy words that are difficult to pronounce comfortably. Simple language and common words work best for scripts.

Figure 11.8

Editing the Video

The piece-to-camera clip is the foundation for the video, but it's the visual sequence that sells the product. The pictures placed above the talking head on the timeline create interest and desire to learn more, and that's the goal of this promotional video.

Exercise

Write a 90-second promo script using the AIDA pattern. Make some test recordings and evaluate the results.

When you're happy with your piece-to-camera take, film shots for a cutaway sequence.

Import and assemble all your footage in a video-editing program that supports multiple video timelines. For example, you can use iMovie, the LumaFusion app, Final Cut Pro, or Adobe Premier.

ONLINE EXAMPLE 11.2

Promoting a Business—Pottery-Making Lessons

This is an example of a video that a small business (like a pottery shop) can produce to promote their business. The feeling is all about what a student experiences during a private lesson.

Building Blocks

The faces of the students were intentionally framed out during filming, and much of the movie was filmed in close-up and slow motion to emphasize the details and dwell on the organic physicality of the process. This anonymity allows the potential customer to project himself or herself into the scene as they begin to imagine themselves doing what they are seeing.

Location

A pottery shop in a Chicago suburb.

Lighting

Available light.

Props

The props seen in the film are the actual tools and materials from the pottery store. No external items were used.

Ethics

All of the filming was done spontaneously and with a free feeling.

Nobody was asked to pose for the camera or repeat his or her actions to make a "second take."

The subjects were simply informed at the beginning that I would be documenting the process and to simply ignore the camera and me.

The sound of the clay hitting the table in the opening sequence is the actual sound recorded as it impacted on the table. This is not a special effect sound added in post-production. The sound became dramatic because it was recorded in slow motion. The pitch is lowered to a thunderous frequency because the sound is also playing back in slow motion. It is a delightful audio artifact that grabs the viewer at the start of the video.

Shooting

Figure 11.9

For each of these sessions I filmed around 30 short clips (less than 10 seconds for each), as well as a number of shots with the built-in camera. These shots were saved to the photo gallery as still frames and also as "live photos." Live photos are a short video clip that late-model iPhones record whenever you snap a picture.

Apps

The apps I used to film were the standard iPhone camera and the slow-mo camera mode set to 240 frames per second. I enabled manual mode by tapping and holding the AE AF lock to get the best focus and exposure.

For a couple of shots I used the Filmic Pro app where I could get even more manual control and I filmed while "pulling focus." The Clips Video Editor by Fly Labs I used to edit this film is no longer available in the app store because a large tech firm in Silicon Valley bought out the developers (see www.theverge. com/2015/11/6/9684530/google-acquires-fly-labs-video-editing). But that doesn't really matter, because you can use a free editing app like the Splice video editor from GoPro or iMovie to get the same result.

Figure 11.10 There were two shooting sessions for this video. The first was when the clay was being molded into the cups and bowls, and the second was when the objects were getting their first applications of color glaze.

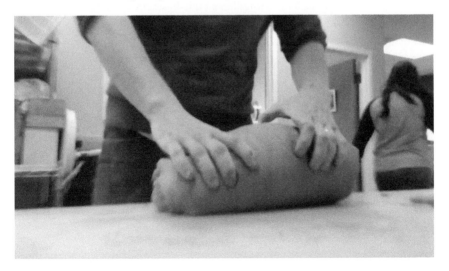

Figure 11.11 The second shot in the film is so violent that it shakes the camera and everything in the room. This sets up a natural transition to the third shot starting out of focus.

Editing the Video

Figure 11.12 You see this effect in the third shot of the film. It begins out of focus.

The shots for this film all fit on a single timeline edit and the only tricky bits were the use of slow-motion shots and a "dream sequence" made up of "live photos."

Live Photos

I built that short video sequence using the Quik video editing app and choosing the "Light" editing preset. This setting has a built-in warming filter and focus crossfades between the shots.

Figure 11.13 I began this edit using the Clips video editor app from On the Fly Labs, which allows me to assemble my shots in a vertical playlist. This is similar to organizing songs in an iTunes playlist.

Figure 11.14 Quik also smartly pulled in the live photos (the short video clips that late-model iPhones record when snapping photos) rather than the still photos. These effects combine nicely when used with care.

Variations

Of course a promotional video for a business doesn't always have to be a music video. I could have interviewed the instructor instead and used his soundbites running underneath the shots. Or I could have put some title cards in between the scenes to explain the process with short teaser texts.

I certainly could have been more formal with the pre-production planning and the coordination with the subjects, but sometimes just chasing a single idea (like filming a process in close-up and in slow motion) can open the door to new ways of promoting an event, issue, persona, course, activity, or business with a video story.

CHAPTER 12

Walkthrough

Provide a narrated tour of an event or location.

Key Concepts

- Voice-over narration
- Shot patterns
- Shot sizes
- Hyperlapse filming
- Neutral framing
- Interviewing

Online Videos

- IFA electronics show
- Hyperlapse tour

Mini Tutorial

- Film like a pro with your smartphone

Exercise

- Film a walkthrough video

Figure 12.1

ONLINE VIDEOS

Watch the videos for this chapter at www.SmartFilmBook.com.

Goal

Produce an informative tour video that needs very little editing.

Challenges

A walkthrough video requires the filmmaker to provide simultaneous voice-over narration while filming a shot pattern. This requires some careful attention to the shot content, the framing, and the words used at the beginning and ending of each clip.

Figure 12.2

ONLINE EXAMPLE 12.1

IFA Electronics Show

This clip provides a sneak peek at new camera gadgets at a consumer electronics show in Berlin.

This walkthrough is one of the first pieces of reporting I made at this event. (You can view the other video reports in the online video package shown in Chapter 1.)

The scene is an exclusive preview party where journalists are invited to see some of the latest gadgets from innovative manufacturers. A walkthrough is an excellent story for this type of occasion, because the viewers will get a sneak peek at new stuff with behind-the-scenes access they would not otherwise have.

In essence, the reporter is serving as a trusted tour guide.

The Shot List

This is the sequence of shots in the lesson video:

1. PTC (outside the venue).
2. POV with narration. (The camera move begins and ends with neutral shot content. This shot transports viewers from outside to inside.)
3. SOUNDBITE—Olloclip guy.
4. NEUTRAL with narration (close-up of drone table—trucking shot).

5. PTC (introduce three new gadgets from one company).
6. SOUNDBITE—Removu guy shows and speaks about gadget 1.
7. CLOSEUP—Reporter summarizes features of gadget 2.
8. SOUNDBITE—Removu guy shows and speaks about gadget 3.
9. NEUTRAL with narration. (Pan from close-up of food to wide shot showing exhibitor's booths.)
10. SOUNDBITE—Olloclip guy with close-up of gadget instead of person.
11. SOUNDBITE—Marshall guy shows smartphone. (Close-up shot size of gadget.)
12. PTC—Summary from reporter.
13. Logo bumper.

KEY

- PTC—Piece-to-camera (a selfie!).
- POV—Point-of-view (what the reporter is seeing).
- SOUNDBITE—Interview responses from a subject.
- NEUTRAL—Neither the reporter nor interview subjects can be seen in the frame. Shots can be entirely neutral from start to finish or neutral framing can be used to open and close any other shot.
- CLOSE-UP—The camera is moved very close to the object to intentionally frame out distractions and to focus on details (no zooming, the camera must be physically as close as possible with focus and exposure locked in manual mode).

Figure 12.3 I arrived at the event early with my phone, grip, headphones, power bank, face light, tripod, and digital lapel microphone.

Pre-production

Figure 12.4 All my gear (except for the tripod) fitted into this small shoulder bag and I set up my rig outside the venue next to a four-person TV crew.

The state broadcaster sent a producer, presenter, camera operator, and a grip who cares for the light and sound.

I decided I would try to compete with them in order to learn what is and isn't possible for one field reporter to produce using only their phone.

I made some practice filming to make sure that the framing for my PTC shot was good, the audio was recording properly, and the face light was working. I had recorded my segment and was inside the venue before the other crew had even finished setting up.

So far, so good.

Location

Messe, Berlin.

Filming the shots

Standing inside the busy scene, I looked for an interesting viewpoint that would connect the outside to the inside. Notice how the shot begins and ends with neutral content. It starts by showing the roof and windows. No people. No reporter. It ends with a neutral framing of an exhibitor's booth. No interview subject is seen.

For my voice-over narration I was thinking of natural transition to introduce the first vendor and interview subject. I did three takes of this shot until I was satisfied.

Figure 12.5 I approached the man at the booth and asked if I could interview him on camera. I simply asked him to tell me a little bit about the new product he's demonstrating.

I filmed some additional cutaway shots at the Olloclip stand before moving through the scene to film some neutral shots that show what else is going on away from the exhibitors' booths. The food was incredible and highly visual, so those shots worked pretty well.

Figure 12.6 I discovered a vendor who had three interesting products that I thought my audience would be interested in learning more about. When it was my turn to talk with the man, I explained to him that I'd like to film him demonstrating his gadgets and to speak a little bit about each one.

To provide some variation and for clarity I used a different framing for each gadget.

The first shot is a medium close-up shot. The second shot is a close-up of his hands and the gadget, and the third shot is of my hand holding the gadget while providing voice-over narration.

That third shot was important because I couldn't get a good soundbite from the subject. This was because he was not very clear in his speech. I asked him if I could summarize what he had just said and he agreed.

I then filmed a few additional neutral shots that show other people at the party.

I found my final interview subject at the Marshall booth speaking about a custom smartphone design.

The framing for this shot is also in close-up with the subject's hands demonstrating the phone's features while he speaks about it. The viewer never actually sees this person's face.

I completed the filming by finding a location that had a decent background and put a little distance between the noisy crowd and me. I adjusted the tripod, turned on my face light, attached the lapel mic, and recorded my summary statement.

Editing the Video

The editing for a walkthrough video recorded with a shot pattern is very straightforward and can be done quickly on the phone.

I used the Clips video editor to cut this reel, but I could have used iMovie or LumaFusion to get the same results.

The finished video pretty much follows the order of the shot sequence I had filmed. I only made a couple small changes. The only fussy work was to trim the beginnings and the endings for each clip and make sure that the narration made sense from start to finish. Because I could assemble the story edit while still at the venue, I could decide then and there if I needed to re-take a scene, or gather additional material.

I added a bumper clip with my branding at the end of the piece. This bumper is a pre-recorded clip I keep in my photo library on my phone.

MINI TUTORIAL

Film Like a Pro With Your Smartphone

1. Get a grip—get close to subjects, pull your arms in, and use a stabilizer (gimbal or tripod) to film steady shots.
2. You sound GREAT!—but be sure and film with an external microphone if you plan on using any sound from the scene. Record interviews in quiet places, far away from loud background noises.
3. Shoot several variations—film the same action in a scene with several shot sizes: wide, medium, close. Use your feet to zoom in closer and not the digital camera zoom.
4. Feel the light—pay attention to when light is too strong and the direction it is coming from. Early morning and late afternoon often produce the best conditions. And also weather can make for dramatic lighting situations, so don't be afraid to film in and around rainy conditions.
5. Film the majority of your video clips between 6 and 10 seconds in length. Your shots will be easier to identify when you begin to edit your video story sequence.

The only difficult part in working with this method as a solo journalist is making sure you maintain continuity with the flow of your narration and that the audio levels are consistent. Oh, and that you remember to film those neutral shots that allow you to seamlessly cut to different people and topics.

Exercise

Film and edit a walkthrough video.

Choose an event or favorite place to feature and scout the location before filming. You can also identify your interview subjects in advance and tell them what you are doing and what you expect.

Use a lapel or stick mic for best audio results.

This is the pattern of shots you can use:

- PTC walking and talking (opening)
- Close-ups with narration
- POV with narration (end on a neutral frame that doesn't show the interview subject)

- Soundbite (introduce your subject, ask a question)
- POV walking with narration (end on a neutral frame)
- Neutral—close-up of badge with narration
- Soundbite (introduce your next subject, ask a question)
- PTC walking and talking (closing)

ONLINE EXAMPLE 12.2

Hyperlapse Tour

This video is made up of a hyperlapse shot of the pressroom with a voice-over narration track.

This is a quick and simple walkthrough style you might also like to experiment with.

Filming the Shot

I used the Hyperlapse by Instagram app to film a walking tour.

Figure 12.7 First, I scouted the scene and identified an opening framing shot of the signage and a closing shot at the coffee bar.

Since a hyperlapse shot is a tracking shot combined with a time-lapse, holding the framing at the beginning and end of the shots is really important. Make sure that for the start and ending framings you film for an extra few seconds in order to allow the viewer to process what they are seeing.

Figure 12.8 Those small, lingering moments on screen provide a nice bookend to the video and help it feel a little more professional.

Editing

I imported the clip into a new iMovie project and went to a quiet place where I could record a voice-over narration with my lapel mic.

It was shot in one take, and I trimmed the clip to 30 seconds and exported the finished video out to my camera roll.